Enlightenment Philosophy

IN A
NUTSHELL

Enlightenment Philosophy

IN A NUTSHELL

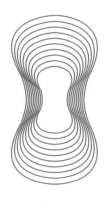

Jane O'Grady

SIRIUS

Acknowledgements

Thank you to my meticulous, intelligent, long-suffering editor at Arcturus, John Turing, and to the wise Vanessa Daubney; to Richard Baron, Andrew Bowie, Bob Clarke, Tony Curzon Price, Alexander Douglas, Mark Fielding, Sacha Golob, John Heyderman, Simon May, Philip Pilkington, Georgia Scoones and Philippa Scoones for giving me (what certainly seemed) excellent advice; to Anna Curzon Price for helping me with the diagrams; Lucy Lethbridge, Prudence Cave, Sibby Curzon Price, Selina O'Grady, Jeremy O'Grady and Carolyn Law for putting up with my kvetching; and all the students that I have taught, or am currently teaching, for their enthusiasm, tolerance and inspiration.

SIRIUS

This edition published in 2018 by Sirius Publishing, a division of Arcturus Publishing Limited,
26/27 Bickels Yard, 151–153 Bermondsey Street,
London SE1 3HA

ISBN: 978-1-78828-583-4
AD006049UK

Printed in China

Contents

Introduction

What is Enlightenment Philosophy?

What is Enlightenment? In 1784, Immanuel Kant wrote an essay answering that question, but it is still being heatedly asked more than two centuries later. Enlightenment from what? From dogma, authority, hierarchy, superstition, religious control and religious intolerance, granted, but was the Enlightenment essentially godless, and how enlightening in fact was it? Who were the enlighteners? Can 'enlightened despots' such as Prussia's Frederick II or Catherine the Great of Russia count as being among them? Was the Enlightenment an integrated, homogeneous movement, or were there as many Enlightenments as there were European countries? Or, as historian Jonathan Israel has recently argued, was it one movement but with two conflicting strands – Radical (anti-traditional) and Moderate (more conservative)? Should the Counter-Enlightenment be considered separate to the Enlightenment, or essential to it, a sign of its complexity and fruitful contradictoriness?

Because when it began is disputed, there isn't even agreement about which European country was its source. Was it

> ### WHAT IS ENLIGHTENMENT?
>
> The question 'What is Enlightenment?' appeared in an exasperated footnote to an article defending marriage and lamenting morality's decline, written in 1783 by a Prussian clergyman, Johann Friedrich Zollner. 'This question, which is nearly as important as "What is truth?"' (he wrote) 'should be answered before one starts to enlighten.' Many intellectuals besides Kant, including Moses Mendelssohn, took up the challenge.

The Enlightenment reached the highest echelons of society, as shown in this image of Louis XIV visiting the Royal Academy of Sciences in Paris.

The Enlightenment ranged from Jonathan Swift's satire (such as Gulliver's Travels, *pictured above) to Immanuel Kant's earnest moral philosophy.*

with Descartes' doubt in the early 17th century? Around 1648 at the end of the 30 Years War? With Spinoza in tolerant Holland, or Newton and Locke in 17th-century England? At the beginning of the 18th century when the French became inspired with 'Anglo-mania'? And when did it end – with the French Revolution in 1789, Kant's death in 1804 or the beginning or end of the Napoleonic Wars? Even given the earliest and latest temporal boundaries, the Enlightenment overflows them back into the Renaissance and forward into Romanticism. It produced a cornucopia of scientific discovery, literature, music, art and architecture as well as philosophy, but it would take several volumes to cover Galileo, Newton, Lavoisier, heliocentrism, the invention of the steam engine, the economics of Beccaria and Adam Smith, the exuberant divinity of Bach, Handel, Haydn and Mozart, the light/dark antithesis, the nudes and portraiture of Rembrandt, Rubens, Vermeer and Velasquez, the ornate emotionality of Baroque churches, the rise of the novel with Defoe and Richardson, and satire from the likes of Jonathan Swift and Voltaire. So how can it be crammed into a nutshell?

It can't, of course, but compression is sometimes handy for communicating the sense of a subject and inspiring further investigation. Only a handful of Enlightenment thinkers can be included, but I hope to show how Descartes, Locke, Spinoza, Berkeley, Hume, Rousseau and Kant respond to, develop, re-form and contradict the ideas of their predecessors and peers such as Hobbes, Leibniz, Hutcheson, Voltaire and Diderot, and in doing so to convey the extraordinary courage and innovativeness of the Enlightenment as a whole.

Each chapter begins with a brief summary of what makes the philosopher it discusses lasting, and ends with a bullet-point summary of the chapter's key ideas. It also gives some details of the philosopher's life, because, as Nietzsche famously said, whereas a scientist or philologist is distinct from their work, philosophy is 'a kind of involuntary and unconscious memoir' of its creator, brewed out of that philosopher's temperament and very essence; the life illustrates and illuminates the philosophy, perhaps especially where the individual's practice conflicts with their theory.

When outlining the ideas of each Enlightenment thinker, I use the present tense, not intending it as a historic present but as an immortal-thought present. Occasionally, where historical context is important, I use the past tense for a philosopher's work, for instance when there needs to be a contrast between what that philosopher used to say, and what he ends up saying, or where I am referring to an earlier thinker whose work he is responding to.

PHILOSOPHERS OF THE ENLIGHTENMENT

René Descartes (1596–1650)

John Locke (1632–1704)

Baruch Spinoza (1632–1677)

George Berkeley (1685–1753)

David Hume (1711–1776)

Jean-Jacques Rousseau (1712–1778)

Immanuel Kant (1724–1804)

Chapter 1

The Road to Enlightenment

In about 600BCE, the Greek citizen Thales asked: 'What is the One underlying the Many?' Until then, human ingenuity had tended to manipulate the world piecemeal – in maths and technology – and to try to explain it as a whole only in terms of myth. Thales' question sprang from the (then) odd and original idea that there must be a single principle (arché) informing and animating the gallimaufry of things in the world, and it made the key distinction that spurs all philosophical and scientific enquiry – the distinction between what things merely *seem* and how they actually *are*.

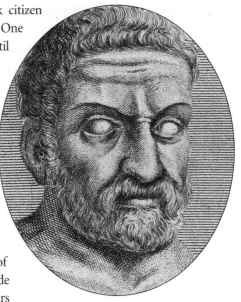

Thales, the first recorded philosopher, asked 'What is the One underlying the Many?'

Soon those who practised what they called philos sophia (love of wisdom) began to turn the spotlight on themselves. They realized that what they investigated was investigated by *them* through the medium of their thought, and of human eyes, skin, ears and other specific sense organs. Philosophy, like science, has always wanted to know what everything is, irrespective of how it seems, but that requires asking 'what or who does everything seem *to*?' We can't winkle ourselves out of our knowing. We have to judge how far, or even if, what we perceive is as we perceive it, and what we believe is true. In the third century BCE, the Skeptikoi (enquirers) questioned whether we can know anything at all – extreme, perhaps, but scepticism is essential to all philosophizing.

THE CRADLE OF ALL SUBJECTS

Philosophy was the cradle of all subjects before any subjects or disciplines had even been identified and differentiated, but gradually the fields of knowledge split off from it as each crystallized round a different basis, perspective, method and topic. The philosophy core that remained split into:

- metaphysics (the study of the nature and structure of reality);
- epistemology (the study of whether, how, and what we know);
- logic;
- aesthetics (the study of art and of what is beautiful);
- ethics; political philosophy and more.

What distinguishes philosophy is not its subject matter but its technique – a perilous mixture of flexible open-endedness and meticulous precision as the philosopher walks a narrow tightrope over undifferentiated chaos, trying to transfix, demarcate and gather it into meaningful concepts, and to make sense also of existing categories and models. A philosopher's tool-kit is him- or herself. Our own *intuitions* (a technical term in philosophy) provide a tuning fork for testing the soundness of what it makes sense to think or say about anything. Yet, while relying on intuitions, philosophy requires us to query all the presuppositions and seeming certainties on which our reasoning is based.

Philosophy is also a conversation, answering, contradicting, building on what other philosophers have said or are saying, and also demolishing it. Indicatively, Descartes, with whom this book begins, and Kant, with whom it ends, both lament how deplorable the current state of philosophy is (in 1641 and 1781 respectively). The appearance/reality distinction had become more puzzling than ever.

THE CENTURIES BETWEEN ARISTOTLE AND DESCARTES

In 380CE, after philosophy's heyday in Athens – and alongside Greek and Roman Stoicism and the neo-Platonists – an initially tiny sect, Christianity, was made the dominant religion of the Roman Empire and was soon the only authorized one. For the next thousand years, religious authority was the bond that united people's thought and action, but also shackled it. Thinking, or its expression, had to be squared with Christian orthodoxy in Europe, and, after 700CE, with Islam in the Middle East and part of Spain.

Of course this is very broad-brush. It is sometimes argued that Christianity itself contained the germ of the Enlightenment. The Christ of the Gospels focuses on what is truly felt and thought as opposed to what is only enacted and said; early Christianity overturned the ancient world's prioritizing of family, nationality, state, hierarchy and convention by insisting on individual conscience. 'There is neither Jew nor Gentile, slave nor free, male nor female, for you are all one in Christ,' said Paul. But Christian 'innerness' and category-transcendence was vitiated by power and rigmarole. 'The Catholic, apostolic and Roman religion is, in all its ceremonies and in all its dogma, the reverse of the religion of Jesus,' Voltaire wrote in the 18th century. The rebirth of pre-Christian Greek and Roman culture in the European Renaissance of the 13th to 16th centuries, Galileo's discovery of the sun being at the universe's centre, Pierre Bayle's provocative *Historical and Critical Dictionary* (dubbed 'the arsenal of the Enlightenment'), the freer pursuit of knowledge, its wider dispersal by means of printing, and the translation of the Bible, were all fiercely suppressed by the Church. Luther's 16th-century Reformation, which was intended to reform it from within, effected a schism, and Catholics fought Protestants in the Holy Roman Empire during a Thirty Years' War in which an estimated eight million people died. In 1648 the Peace of Westphalia drew up a series of treaties stipulating that from now on each region would adopt the religion of its ruler, though with members of minority religions having the right to practise their faith. It was futile for Pope Innocent X to pronounce the treaties 'null, void, invalid, iniquitous, unjust, damnable, reprobate, inane, empty of meaning and effect for all time'. Protestant factions had been officially recognized, and any chance for the Catholic reconquest of Europe obliterated.

A GENERAL
DICTIONARY,
Hiſtorical and Critical:
IN WHICH

A New and Accurate **TRANSLATION**
of that of the Celebrated

Mr. BAYLE,

WITH THE

CORRECTIONS and **OBSERVATIONS** printed
in the late Edition at *Paris*, is included ; and interſperſed
with ſeveral thouſand **LIVES** never before publiſhed.

The whole containing the Hiſtory of the moſt illuſtrious Perſons of all Ages
and Nations, particularly thoſe of *Great Britain* and *Ireland*, diſtinguiſhed
by their Rank, Actions, Learning and other Accompliſhments.

With Reflections on ſuch Paſſages of Mr. BAYLE, as ſeem to favour *Scepticiſm* and
the *Manichee* Syſtem.

By the Reverend Mr. **JOHN PETER BERNARD**;
The Reverend Mr. **THOMAS BIRCH**;
Mr. **JOHN LOCKMAN**;
And other HANDS.

And the Articles relating to **ORIENTAL HISTORY**
By **GEORGE SALE**, Gent.

VOLUME I.

LONDON,

Printed by *James Bettenham,*

For G. STRAHAN, J. CLARKE, T. HATCHET in *Cornhill*; J. GRAY in the *Poultry*; J. BATLEY
in *Pater-Noſter-Row*; T. WORRALL, J. SHUCKBURGH in *Fleetſtreet*; J. WILCOX, A. MILLAR,
C. CORBET in the *Strand*; T. OSBORNE in *Grays-Inn*; J. BRINDLEY in *New Bond-ſtreet*;
and C. WARD and R. CHANDLER at the *Ship* between the Temple Gates in *Fleetſtreet*, and ſold
at their Shop in SCARBOROUGH.

MDCCXXXIV.

The Historical and Critical Dictionary *was dubbed
'the arsenal of the Enlightenment'.*

WHY – AND WHAT?

Fragmentation of the religious monolith, weariness at fatuous bloodshed over minute religious distinctions, revelatory scientific discoveries, social factors such as capitalism and greater class flexibility – these were some of the factors that led to scepticism of authority and an upsurge of new ideas. Protestantism of all sorts demanded a direct relationship between human and God, rejecting the priest as essential middleman. If reason was, as Augustine had called it in the fourth century, 'the inner light of God', then why should priests, religious strictures, tradition, or even the Bible, be final arbiters of thought? Surely you should side-step them and rely on reason alone. 'Enlightenment is man's emergence from his self-imposed immaturity,' is the first sentence of Kant's essay on Enlightenment – 'self-imposed' because of what Kant considers our 'laziness and cowardice' in failing to think for ourselves without being guided by others. 'If I have a book to understand for me, a pastor to serve as my conscience, a doctor to decide my diet, and so on, I need not exert myself at all. I need not think, if I can only pay.'

Enlightenment thinkers were trying to do what the Ancient Greeks had done: think from first principles, and persuade everyone else to do so too. They urged criticism of all beliefs and ideas, including their own, and the promulgation of new ones. The multi-volume *Encyclopedia*, edited by Diderot and d'Alembert, had gathered free-thinking experts in different fields to collectively summarize all extant knowledge, thereby counteracting the orthodoxies of church and state.

Of course the *Encyclopedia* was censored and shut down, just as Galileo had felt forced to recant his theories in front of the Inquisition, Descartes had needed to suppress his *Treatise of the World*; and books by Enlightenment thinkers were constantly banned and burned, their authors imprisoned or banished from their cities or countries. But 'a lively fermentation of minds', as d'Alembert put it, was 'spreading through nature in all directions like a river that has burst its dams', and it 'swept with a sort of violence everything along with it which stood in its way'.

Whatever else, the Enlightenment can never be seen as one of those movements that was named and concocted retrospectively. It was triumphantly self-conscious. 'Aufklarung' and 'Siecle des lumières' were names current in the 18th century ('Enlightenment' wasn't used until the 19th), and they signalled the namers' determination to pursue science, philosophy and political improvement in the light of reason. Enlightenment thinkers unanimously saw themselves as throwing off the shackles of religious and state authority. Even revisionists who insist that the 'Dark Ages' had their own sort of light would admit that great thinkers such as Augustine, Abelard and Aquinas had been constrained by the need to examine religious questions and not exceed prescribed Christian boundaries, and that for the thousand years preceding Enlightenment, philosophy had been the handmaiden to theology.

Montesquieu established the principle of the separation of powers between the three branches of state: the legislature, the executive and the judiciary.

It was life in this world, rather than in the questionable next, that was now, in the 17th century, the focus of thought, the criterion for change. Spinoza, Locke, Rousseau and others, all in very different ways, urged religious tolerance, free speech and political freedom. Montesquieu's *Spirit of the Laws* advocated a freedom-enhancing separation between the state's legislative, executive and judicial powers. Locke, Hobbes and Rousseau, in their different ways, contended that any state's legitimacy could only be based on a social contract, which ensured the rational consent of the ruled. So much for the Divine Right of Kings.

And why harp on humanity's fallenness, our natural propensity to evil? Hutcheson, Shaftesbury, Hume and Adam Smith all variously argued that humans possess an instinctive sympathy towards one another, which alone serves as the foundation of morality, thus dispensing with any appeal to divine command. 'Our hopes for the future condition of the human race may be summed up in three important points', wrote the political scientist the Marquis de Condorcet, 'the elimination of the inequality between nations; progress in equality within each nation; and the true perfection of mankind.' The Enlightenment was (and still should be) a project. 'If we are asked, "Do you now live in an *enlightened age*?"' wrote Kant, 'the answer is, "No, but we do live in an *age of enlightenment*."'

Voltaire, like many Enlightenment thinkers, was a Deist and practised natural religion.

HOW SECULAR, PAGAN AND ANTI-CLERICAL WAS THE ENLIGHTENMENT?

Probably more Enlightenment thinkers than admitted to it were atheist or agnostic. Even Hume thought it prudent to prevaricate, although heretically declaring that 'the Christian religion not only was at first attended with miracles, but even at this day cannot be believed by any reasonable person without one'. Spinoza anticipated Strauss and other 19th-century scholars by scrutinizing the Bible's authenticity. Voltaire, with his famous signature exhortation '*Écrasez l'infâme!*' ('Crush the vileness!'), fought the injustices of the Catholic Church, and Diderot endorsed the wish attributed to Jean Meslier, a secretly atheist priest: 'Let us strangle the last king with the guts of the last priest.'

But many Enlightenment thinkers, including Voltaire, were Deists and believed in natural (as opposed to revealed) religion. And while Spinoza's 'God' was everything (therefore possibly nothing), Descartes, Berkeley and Leibniz continued to profess some form of Christianity –

indeed God was an essential part of their metaphysics. Leibniz, a strange mixture of the old and new, argued that God is the 'sufficient or final reason' for everything existing, from whose 'supreme perfection' the best of all possible worlds must (of moral necessity) proceed. He coined the term 'theodicy' ('justifying God'), and in his essay of this title tackled the problem of how a good God can allow metaphysical and moral evil.

DEISM

Deism is a set of views which hold that, although God exists and has created the world, He is not a personal intercessor in human life. Deists disavow divine revelation, prophets and sacred texts.

For many, belief in God was shaken by the Lisbon earthquake of 1755, which could hardly be blamed on sinners as it mainly hit worshippers in the cathedral, sparing the seedy prostitute-frequented areas of the city. Voltaire wrote a poetic lament. Rousseau answered it with a letter sneering at such facile pessimism. Voltaire's response to both Rousseau and Leibniz was his famous novel *Candide*, in which the protagonists undergo the most excruciating sufferings, throughout which the eponymous hero's tutor, Dr Pangloss, always insists that this is the best of all possible worlds, even after he has been almost burned, and then hung, to death, semi-dissected, lashed and made a galley-slave.

'If God did not exist, it would be necessary to invent him' is a famous quotation from Voltaire; but he thought that even though God did exist, He needed to be invented all the same, because unknowable. 'If God has made us in his image, we have returned him the favour.'

THE LEGACY OF THE ENLIGHTENMENT

At the time and for long afterwards, the Enlightenment was glorified by progressive thinkers and vilified by reactionaries, some of whom blamed it, as Hegel did, for inspiring not only the French Revolution but the Terror. But now the Enlightenment is often condemned by the left, and seen as the provenance of the right. This trend perhaps began in 1944 when Adorno and other members of the left-wing Frankfurt School criticised Enlightenment thinkers for over-adulating reason and promoting the domination of nature, both of which (according to Adorno) had been conducive to Nazism. It has been exacerbated by the identity politics which upholds disadvantaged groups (such as women, ethnic minorities, the disabled and LGBTQ people) whose viewpoints are considered to have been lost or ignored in the Enlightenment's celebration of universal reason and universal improvement. Enlightenment's alleged universalism is dismissed as disrespectfully oblivious to the variety of moral and human frameworks, and a mask for eurocentrism, colonization, racism and Western interventionism.

But it was precisely exploitation, eurocentrism and racism that the Enlightenment was attacking, and the plight of women, the colonized and slaves that it was dedicated to improving, even if not sufficiently strongly or consistently. For the diversity of cultures to be celebrated, it was first necessary that they were not belittled or vilified – that the assumed exclusivity and superiority that European, and other cultures, assumed to themselves be transcended, and respect extended to all. Enlightenment universalism was what enabled the very identity politics that now condemns it. It is a victim of its own success and of the incessant critiquing that was so essential to it, which made its thinkers scorpion round to sting their own ideas. A constant hero in Enlightenment fiction was the foreigner (African, Persian, Abyssinian or Huron Indian) through whose eyes we see the faults and foibles of Paris, provincial France, or wherever they visit. The crabbed prudishness and hypocrisy of European sexual mores is shown up by the happy unrestraint of the Tahitians in Diderot's *Supplement to the Voyage of Bougainville*. Leibniz, an avid student of Chinese culture, said Europe needed missionaries from China because of the superiority of Chinese ethics and politics.

Enlightenment thinkers saw themselves as 'citizens of the world', yet, oddly, many on the present-day left would probably agree with the reactionary aristocrat Joseph de Maistre, who objected that the Republican constitution of 1795 'has been drawn up for Man', and that 'a constitution that is made for all nations is made for none'. For de Maistre averred that, although in the course of his life he had come across Frenchmen, Italians, Russians, even (thanks to Montesquieu's *Persian Letters*) Persians, he had never met Man – 'there is no such thing in the world'. Some supporters of identity politics similarly deny that

The Native American was a common feature of Enlightenment fiction. He was used to show up the flaws of European society as well as celebrated for his own presumed merits, as shown in Benjamin West's famous painting The Death of General Wolfe.

The French Terror, beginning in 1793, arguably marked the end of the Enlightenment, when a large number of the philosophes were executed.

there can be any general 'human' interests, any more, they say, than there can be truth. 'Truth' (in inverted commas, of course) is said to be the construction of dead white males, whose power it serves and promotes.

This objection is itself a product of Enlightenment, perhaps an overdevelopment of one of its tenets. There is something anachronistic in the way *Sapere aude* (Kant's declared motto of Enlightenment) is so often translated as 'Dare to think for yourself', when its accurate translation is 'dare to know'. Enlightenment thinkers advocated challenging accepted 'truths' because these had got in the way of seeking truth. Thinking for yourself was important, not for its own sake, but, rather, as a means to an end. They hoped and expected that subjective reasonings would ultimately converge on objective truth.

Ironically, the exhortation to free thinking has been exaggerated and distorted into the notion that all opinions are important and equally valid, and also into that of Moral Relativism – which in fact is inconsistent with it, for it encourages the return to group-think within cultural boundaries and to the pious acceptance of tradition and rigmarole that Enlightenment was precisely dedicated to subverting. Yet those such as Richard Dawkins and Sam Harris, who, in the name of Enlightenment, condemn religion wholesale, are insensitive to the nuances and significance of religious faith which Enlightenment thinkers themselves appreciated. They too go against the spirit of Enlightenment.

Of course things were written then that we might disapprove of now, but it is anachronistic to expect people living about 300 years ago to share our views – and absurdly inconsistent from the very people who preach relativism and condone geographically localized barbarisms.

Those who hurriedly proclaim that Islamist terrorists are not, whatever the terrorists themselves claim, true Muslims – that their very atrocities disqualify them – should surely apply the same reasoning to evils done in the name of Enlightenment. As well as *Sapere aude*, 'Liberty, Equality, Fraternity' could also have been the slogan of Enlightenment as of the French Revolution, which, arguably, it inspired.

FROM REASON TO NATURALISM

The Enlightenment is sometimes accused of exalting reason at the expense of emotion and everyday life. Romanticism, with its glorification

'We hold these truths to be self-evident, that **all men are created equal,** that they are endowed by their Creator with certain unalienable Rights, that among these are Life, Liberty and the pursuit of Happiness.'

The American Declaration of Independence, July 4 1776

'The sun will rise only upon a world of free men who will recognize no master other than their own reason, where tyrants and slaves, priests and their stupid and hypocritical instruments, will exist only in history or in the theatre . . . we will have seen reason emerge victorious from that struggle, so long and so painful, so that at last we will be able to write: truth has triumphed; the human race is saved.'

Marquis de Condorcet, 1793 (the same year he was branded a traitor, despite all his work for the Revolution. He died in prison in 1794 under mysterious circumstances.)

of 'feeling' and the wild, is said to have been the reaction to over-intellectualizing. But although the Enlightenment era is called the Age of Reason, in a way it adulated reason less than the eras before it had done. In Christian Europe, reason, although forced to subserve religious dogma, had been honoured as the essence of a human's semi-divinity, and seen as intrinsic to the world. Most medievals would have agreed with Aristotle that animals, because they 'have neither the faculty of choice nor of calculation . . . are aberrations from nature, like men who are insane'. Humans were, as Dante's Ulysses urged his mariners to remember, 'not made to live like beasts, but to follow virtue and knowledge'. As late as 1729, Alexander Pope wrote that 'Nature, like Liberty, is but restrain'd/ By the same Laws which first herself ordain'd', echoing Stoicism's notion of a rationally ordered world in which humans would rationally fit, were they not distracted by involuntary emotion.

Thanks to the Enlightenment, with its experimental science and rational critique, nature could no longer be seen as God's Book or humans as part of the Great Chain of Being. Emotion, although sometimes still dismissed as superfluous, was more often regarded as intrinsically valuable and potentially ennobling, a substitute for divine command. Perfection of emotion and character were importantly included in the Enlightenment project of perfecting humankind. Though a rationalist, Descartes declared that those most deeply moved by emotion were 'capable of enjoying the sweetest pleasures of this life'. Analysis of emotion had been 'meagre' and 'implausible' until now, he said, and belonged in the realm of science, not of moral philosophy. If emotions had always been distinguished from reason, so much the worse for reason. Although it was the hub of Kant's moral system, in that of Sentimentalists such as Hutcheson and Shaftesbury, or of Hume, it was demoted in favour of sympathy and fellow-feeling.

The backlash against reason which led to Romanticism was in fact part of the Enlightenment itself. In the very act of dethroning superstition and authority, and crowning human dignity and freedom of thought, reason began the discovery of how insignificant and irrational humans really are. Elevating humans and human reason led to downgrading both. Instead of having been made especially for us, the world turned out to be merely one of many planets circling the sun. Reason itself is just an animal instinct, said Hume, and the naturalizing that he and Rousseau began would ultimately put humans, the supposed transcenders of nature, on all fours with 'the beasts'. The notion of perfectibility would be junked.

The fabulous fecundity of the Enlightenment was the gateway to modern bleakness – to Freud, who would see reason as a specious gloss over our wild unconscious desires, and to Darwin, who would show us to be glorified apes. It was the beginning of what Weber called 'the disenchantment of the world' in which divinity would be stripped away, not just from the cosmos, but from ourselves. And, arguably, it ended with the violent irrationality of the Terror, in which rational *philosophes* were executed, or (perhaps) with the colonising Napoleonic Wars that followed.

LES PHILOSOPHES

The model philosopher was once the Stoic. But the 'philosopher' entry in the *Encyclopedia* declared that 'the true philosopher', far from being an abstemious recluse, is a free-thinker who engages in public affairs and in pleasure, who 'forms his convictions only by evidence'. The term *'philosophe'* – flaunted by the French intellectual coterie, and often derided by outsiders – took on its own specialised meaning.

Philosophes were more than philosophers. Setting out 'to comprehend everything', they were dilettantes in all disciplines, including 'natural philosophy' (science). Lacking systematically accumulated research and sophisticated equipment, they had to invent their own scientific methodology. 'This is my book', Descartes (a proto-*philosophe*) is reported to have said, pointing to a calf that he was dissecting in his equivalent to a laboratory, the courtyard behind his Amsterdam house. Leibniz, little of whose philosophy was published during his lifetime, discovered binary arithmetic, invented the calculus, designed water pumps, mining machines, water desalination systems, submarines and an early steam engine; proposed ideas for insurance schemes; reformed coinage; and was innovative in physics, chemistry, medicine, botany, philology, geology and architecture. Voltaire was the first populariser of science, along with his mistress Emilie du Chatelet, whose translation of Newton's *Principia* (which remains its only French version) came out in 1749, the year she died in giving birth to a baby that was not Voltaire's.

'*Les philosophes* were not philosophers', said an American philosopher in the early 20th century. Perhaps not, if we hold them to the pristine consistency and narrow rigour of Anglo-American analytic philosophy. But to do so is to miss Voltaire's ambiguous wit, the rich contradictoriness of Hume (he was an honorary *philosophe* in Paris), and the polymathic proflicness of so many of them. The *philosophes* were not academics but activists, dedicated to promoting unfettered enquiry, and parrying persecution by Church and state. By 1782 Rousseau's revelatory *Confessions* could be published. In 1641, Descartes gave his daring speculations a title that cautiously identified them with the solitary meditations undertaken by pious Catholics. Earlier, in his notebooks, he had written: 'In this theatre which is the world, ... I am now about to mount the stage, and I come forward masked.'

Chapter 2

René Descartes (1596–1650)

René Descartes is celebrated as the father of modern philosophy and for writing the famous philosophical sentence: 'I think therefore I am.' A founding figure of Enlightenment, he changed the nature not just of philosophy but of learning itself. By deposing the authority of the Bible, Aristotle and accepted thought, he made the thinking individual both starting-point and final judge of all enquiry. Largely thanks to him, epistemology (the study of how, what, if we can know) replaced metaphysics as the main focus in philosophy for the next 250 years. Rightly

Descartes changed the nature of philosophy by deposing the authority of both the Bible and classical thinkers.

considered a **rationalist** (someone for whom reason is the ultimate arbiter of truth), Descartes hugely influenced **empiricists** (for whom all knowledge is derived from sensory experiences); he made thinking itself an experience and reason a process.

A SCIENTISTIC WORLD-VIEW

Descartes was also a pioneering scientist. His mathematical innovations inspired Leibniz's and Newton's discovery of calculus; he invented the graph and founded analytical geometry; helped to lay the foundation for the theory of dynamics; formulated the concepts of 'momentum' and the conservation of energy; pioneered optics and discovered the law of refraction; and was fruitfully wrong in his theories on the rainbow and the circulation of blood. His physics was soon to be superseded by Newton's, and his scientific discoveries have been somewhat submerged, but his 'mechanical philosophy' effectively gave us the scientistic world-view we have now – of a universe that consists of atoms endlessly combining, dispersing and recombining, in which thoughts, feelings, sensations, and even colours, sounds, smells and tastes, have a subjective, almost illusory, status. Cartesian dualism, the distinction between mental and physical, is named after him – not that he originated it, but he rendered it more scientific precisely by outlawing the mental from science. How – or indeed whether – mind fits into nature has been for some time philosophy's most insoluble and burning issue.

Descartes was born on 31 March 1596, into a middle-class Catholic family in Touraine in central France. After taking a law degree at Poitiers University, in 1616 he abandoned study for 'the great book of the world'

SUBJECTIVE AND OBJECTIVE IDEAS

'Subjective' and 'objective' are terms used relatively to one another. In law especially, 'subjective' can mean 'biased and self-interested' as opposed to 'impartial'. Hence 'subjective' can also mean 'being so individual as to be illusory (in contrast to what is actually the case)'.

Ever since Descartes, a subjective idea (see p.41) is one that:

1) **Is accessible to only one person;**

2) **Cannot exist independent of observation (by that one person).**

As opposed to something (objective) that:

1) **Is accessible to more than one person;**

2) **Can exist independently of being observed.**

– travelling in Europe, visiting foreign courts, joining Prince Maurice of Nassau's army in the Netherlands at the outbreak of the Thirty Years War (where he was more occupied in military engineering than in fighting) and even (some say) spying for the Catholic Church. A loner who relished solitary unrestricted freedom, he followed his nose for knowledge wherever it took him, 'reflecting upon whatever came [his] way so as to derive some profit from it'.

Typically, it was because he happened to see a mathematical puzzle on a billboard in a Flemish town, and to ask the nearest bystander to translate it into French or Latin for him, that he met and made friends with the mathematician Isaac Beeckman in 1618. 'Roused from [his] state of indolence', he became more focused on studying maths and science, although his travelling and soldiering continued.

In November 1619, shut up alone in a stove-heated room while billeted in a small German town, Descartes spent a whole day meditating, then went to bed heady with ideas and had a night of vivid dreams. According to his earliest biographer, he dreamed that he was assailed by phantoms, spun around by a whirlwind, continually knocked off his feet while those around him walked upright; offered a melon from some exotic country; woke, and was painfully struck in the side, perhaps by an evil demon; dreamed again, and was woken by a deafening thunderclap to see his room bristling with fiery sparks; finally dreamed of finding a dictionary on his table (which disappeared, then later reappeared no longer complete) and a poetry collection in which he read the opening of Ausonius's ode: 'What road in life shall I follow?' About 300 years later, Freud was invited to analyse these dreams, but sensibly demurred. Descartes' interpretation was that he had been divinely appointed to reform human knowledge (and also his previously dissolute life).

Reformation in learning was indeed necessary. Medieval universities were dominated by Scholasticism – a blend of Aristotle and Christianity, reason and faith. Descartes was defiantly opposed to Aristotle, or rather to the Scholastics' version of him. So would Aristotle himself be, if resurrected, said Descartes. He scorned the 'mediocre minds' that twined round these old texts 'like ivy'. Producing endless commentaries, but failing to tackle new problems, they were only 'aspiring to be philosophers', and were in effect historians. Descartes saw himself as

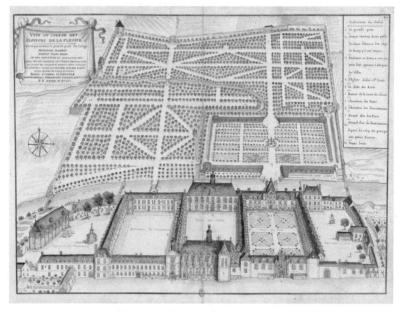

Descartes was educated by the Jesuits at the famous college of La Flèche.

'opening windows and admitting daylight' into a darkened cellar. The correct method of philosophising, he asserted in *Rules for the Direction of the Mind* (written in 1628, published posthumously) was to 'investigate what we can clearly and evidently intuit or deduce with certainty, and not what other people have thought or what we ourselves conjecture'.

For Descartes, as for the Presocratics, philosophy comprised all branches of knowledge, metaphysics being merely the roots, with epistemology – which is what we most remember him for – presumably just root-tips. It looms large for us, because we look at Descartes and his legacy through time's telescope, but for him was only the preliminary to setting out his multi-disciplinary account of the world. 'I have resolved to explain all the phenomena of nature, i.e. all of physics,' he wrote in a letter about *The World*, the book he was writing between 1629 and 1633; it tackled the origin of the universe, cosmology, fire, heat, light, the sea, hardness and liquidity, sensations, perception and the human body.

For all his audacity, though, Descartes was careful to tailor his work to fit in with Catholic teaching. In *The World* he presented the earth

'The whole of philosophy is like a tree. The roots are metaphysics, the trunk is physics, and the branches emerging from the trunk are all the other sciences, which may be reduced to three principal ones, namely medicine, mechanics and morals.'

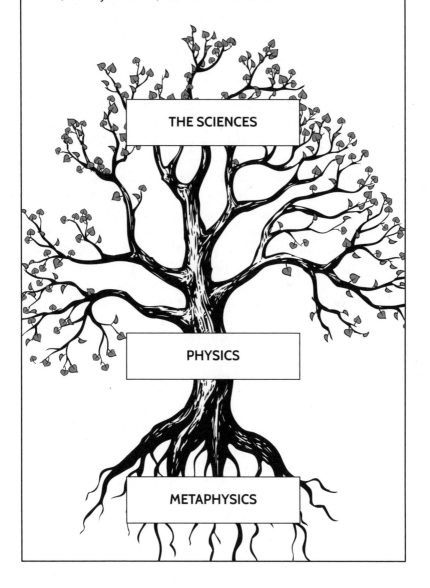

THE SCIENCES

PHYSICS

METAPHYSICS

as 'strictly speaking' motionless and its revolution around the sun as 'hypothetical' (a wink to the cognoscenti). And when, just as the book was about to be published in 1633, he heard that Galileo had been summoned to appear before the Inquisition, he stopped publication. 'It is not my temperament to set sail against the wind,' he said.

Descartes' first published work was brought out anonymously in 1637: *The Discourse on the Method of Rightly Conducting One's Reason and Seeking the Truth in the Sciences*, an introduction to three essays: *Optics, Geometry and Meteorology* (containing some innocuous parts of *The World*). *The Discourse*, which mingled autobiography, metaphysics, physics and medicine, was where the famous 'Je pense, donc je suis' first appeared; but it was *Geometry*, with its novel combination of algebra and geometry, that proved most controversial. In 1641, *Meditations on First Philosophy* was published under his name.

Acquiring fame interfered with Descartes' desire for unfettered solitude (he kept moving house to avoid visits from admirers). He became embroiled in a five-year-long vituperative correspondence with the rector of Utrecht University, Gisbert Voetius, who had accused him of promulgating atheism. A more productive correspondence was with Princess Elisabeth of Bohemia. *Principles of Philosophy*, which combines metaphysics and science, was dedicated to her in 1644.

It was at the princess's request that Descartes wrote about 'the passions', as emotions were then called. He was probably emotional himself. When his illegitimate daughter died aged five, he wrote: 'I am not one of those who think that tears and sadness are appropriate only for women, and that to appear a stout-hearted man one must force oneself to put on a calm expression at all times.' Other letters reveal extreme anger and envy. *The Passions of the Soul* (1649) provides psychologically astute examples, but clumsily attempts to annex common sense to science. Descartes relies on the theory of 'animal spirits' (first postulated in the third century, and persisting till the 19th), according to which very fine fibres, or perhaps air, flicker through the body from brain to muscles, thus enabling us to move. He succeeds in being only pseudoscientific, and in highlighting problems in his theory of mind.

In 1649 Descartes went to Sweden at the repeated invitation of Queen Christina of Sweden. Autumn and winter were cold and dark in

Descartes maintained a learned correspondence with Princess Elisabeth of Bohemia for several years.

Stockholm. Descartes had to get up uncongenially early and stand bare-headed while he taught the Queen. When the French ambassador, his friend, was ill, Descartes nursed him, caught pneumonia, and died aged 53 on 11 February, 1650. Despite his circumspection, several of his works were put on the Catholic Index of Forbidden Books after his death.

FROM DOUBT TO CERTAINTY IN THE MEDITATIONS

Descartes' most famous work, *The Meditations on First Philosophy*, was written between 1638 and 1640 and published in 1641. Consisting of six chapters (six meditations), it was dedicated to the clerics at the Sorbonne, with careful assurances that it would bolster belief in God and the immortal soul. Perhaps as a form of marketing, Descartes had invited criticisms of the book from leading thinkers, including the English philosopher Thomas Hobbes; these Objections, along with Descartes' Replies to them, were incorporated in the work on publication. Soon afterwards, the complete text was translated into French, following Descartes' ethos of popularizing knowledge beyond the world of Latin-speaking scholars.

Descartes was determined to start from the foundations and rebuild a properly secure edifice of human knowledge. First, he says, 'I will devote myself sincerely and without reservation to the general demolition of my opinions.' The 'I' here and throughout the *Meditations* is not 'I, Descartes' but a sort of Every-I (like the Everyman in medieval plays) who is invited to travel with him on this pilgrimage from scepticism to new certainties. The reader is made privy to Descartes' meditations and encouraged to undertake his (or improbably her) own.

Three Stages of Doubt (Meditation 1 to 2)

Descartes sets out to doubt everything he (I) has ever believed. He does this in three stages, with each doubt being answered, only to be replaced by a further, deeper doubt.

1) Descartes doubts the evidence of his senses. Ever since the sceptics in the third century BCE, it had been a moot point how much the senses are our portals on reality, and how much they (in the quaint philosophical personification) 'deceive us', as when we have optical illusions or hallucinations, or distant objects look tiny. If, runs the reasoning, we know that *sometimes* we have false sensory perceptions, how can we be sure that we ever perceive accurately at all?

Answer: To disbelieve that I am now sitting by the fire in my dressing-gown would be as crazy as believing that I am a pumpkin or made of glass.

2) Yes, but this could all be a dream. If I am dreaming that I feel the fire's warmth and see its brightness, then I would feel and see exactly as I am now feeling and seeing. Again: if *sometimes* x, y, z, then maybe *always* x, y, z.

Answer: That's possible, but even in dreams there are some indubitable things: 2 + 3 = 5, for instance, is always true. (Descartes is referring to ineluctable numerical concepts, not to the way numbers are drawn, written or spoken, which could be changed.) The colours and shapes we dream, and even fantasy creatures, are concocted from real things we have encountered in our waking lives.

3) OK, but suppose that (to use a metaphor that Descartes could not have used) we are hard-wired to be mistaken even about mathematics and logic.

Even fantasy creatures are composed out of things we have come across in our waking lives.

Answer: Doffing his cap to his dedicatees, the clerics at the Sorbonne, Descartes hastily says: of course I have always believed in an all-powerful God, Who, because He is also totally good, would not deceive me. But after all, I have sometimes been deceived (by my senses and in dreams) – so just suppose that I had instead been created by a malin genie *(usually translated 'evil demon'), who is wholly dedicated to misleading me.*

Postulating the evil demon finally enables Descartes to totally doubt everything he's ever believed: God, the earth, the sky, any living or non-living thing of any kind, even him and his memories and maths. Perhaps there never was a René Descartes who was born in 1596 (here you can substitute your own name and birth-date). Perhaps anything that he thinks he remembers is false, and his body is an illusion. 'So

Descartes is enabled to doubt absolutely everything – by postulating an evil demon dedicated to misleading him.

what remains true? Perhaps just the one fact that nothing is certain.'

Descartes is not supposing that there *is* an evil demon. It is invoked, not as a creator-god that might exist, but as a method of suggesting that 'I' (Descartes and me) may be being systematically and totally duped; in which case, it really is impossible to believe anything. (Descartes needs the passive voice, as in 'the teapot is broken' rather than 'I broke the teapot'.)

Descartes' U-turn: 'The Sticking Point' (Meditation 2)

But isn't there *something* that is undoubtable? Perhaps there is a God who is causing me to have the thoughts I'm having?
No, since I myself could be the originator of my thoughts. Yet:

1) If my thoughts are caused by me, then I at least must be something.
But how could I be anything? According to what I've just been supposing, the senses are wholly deceptive and I have no senses and no body.

2) Am I so inextricably bound up with senses and body that without them I couldn't exist?
Well, I've just convinced myself that absolutely nothing exists: no world, no sky, no minds, no bodies.

3) Yes, but if *I* was being convinced (of nothingness) – in fact if I've been thinking anything at all – then I (whatever 'I' may be) must be existing (or how could I *be* convinced, or think?)
But there may be an evil demon (extremely powerful) who is deceiving me.

4) OK, but I who am being deceived must therefore be something –

5) 'And let [the evil demon] deceive me as much as he likes, he will never bring it about that I am nothing so long as I think that I am something.'

So I cannot be mistaken in thinking that I am *something* (the something that is producing thoughts, being convinced, perhaps being deceived), even though it is still a moot point what on earth I could be.

Ultimately then I have to conclude that '"I am, I exist" is necessarily true whenever it is put forward by me or conceived in my mind'. Or, as Descartes puts it in *Discourse on the Method*, 'ego cogito, ergo ego sum' – 'I think, therefore I am.'

Student: How do I know that I exist?

Teacher (philosopher Sidney Morgenbesser): Who's asking?

Rebutting the cogito

There are various ways of trying to rebut 'the cogito', as Descartes' argument is called.

1) Some people's immediate response is to say, 'Descartes must have had a brain in order to think, so why does he make thinking the "proof" of existing?' That is to misunderstand what Descartes is doing, which is to clear the decks and start from scratch. For the purposes of this thought experiment, he is holding at arm's length all his knowledge of human anatomy and biology, along with his memories, experiences, bodily feelings, perceptions and all of his presuppositions; he is strenuously trying to doubt them. But, as he says in the *Meditations*' synopsis, 'No sane person has ever seriously doubted these things.'

2) The 'therefore' in the cogito suggests that it is a syllogistic deduction, with the (implicit) form:

'Everything which thinks is, or exists.
I think.
Therefore I exist.'

Descartes, however, denied that he was deducing. 'When we observe that we are thinking beings, this is a sort of primary notion, which is not the conclusion of any syllogism. When someone says "I am thinking, therefore I am, or I exist", he does not deduce existence from thought by means of a syllogism, but recognizes it as something self-evident by a simple intuition of the mind.'

Pierre Gassendi wondered why 'I walk therefore I am' could not do the same job as 'I think therefore I am'.

3) For all his proclaimed ditching of presuppositions, Descartes nonetheless presupposes a publicly available language in which to say or write 'I think therefore I am', and thus a world of other thinkers and speakers, in advance of the 'I'. But couldn't a public language be part of the grand deception?

4) In one of his Objections, Pierre Gassendi testily asked why 'ambulo ergo sum' (I walk therefore I am) would not do just as well as 'cogito ergo sum'. But oddly enough, walking is not as immediate and incontrovertible as thinking, given the expanded sense of 'thinking' that Descartes is determined to introduce. You could after all be dreaming, or hallucinating, or hypnotized to imagine, that you are walking. What is certain, however, is that you are *thinking* you are walking.

All Descartes needs to establish is the act and event of thinking; what the thinking is *about* is irrelevant. He does, though, seem to need an extra thought, so as to wheel round and catch himself thinking, or having just thought.

5) Hyperaspistes (the pseudonym of another Objector) objected: 'You do not know whether it is you yourself who think, or whether the world-soul in you thinks, as the Platonists believe.'

6) All Descartes has proved is that 'There are thoughts (about doubting, the evil demon, being deceived, etc.)'. It is only grammatically that thoughts require a thinker. His reasoning gets only as far as '*it* thinks', but never makes it to '*I* think'.

Thought as form, thought as content

'Thought' has two meanings, which overlap but which are often misleadingly conflated. Thought 1 is a one-off mental event that occurs at a particular point in time, and is 'had' by a particular person; is private and subjective; is caused by (some say, is also identical with) the firing of neurons in someone's brain. Thought 2 is what the action or event of thinking (Thought 1) is *about*; is (metaphorically) *what is contained* by Thought 1. Impersonal, in the public domain, unanchored to time – something expressible in a sentence within a common language, and potentially translatable into other languages.

When I was a child, adults would say, 'A penny for your thoughts.' What they paid for was not the act of thinking I had just done, or the just-finished firing of neurons in my brain, but a sentence that could be written or spoken, or for that matter thought, by anyone. Similarly, you phone someone to say, 'I was just thinking: it's such a beautiful day – let's have a picnic.' They reply, 'That's amazing; I was just having the same thought myself.' They had in fact been having the same Thought 2, but could not have had the same Thought 1.

It is the event of thinking, not the content of thought, that is the important thing. By itself, Thought 2 is just a sentence in the public language. But when I find myself thinking (the potentially free-floating) Thought 2, then Thought 2 is localized to its container (Thought 1) – in me. And through finding myself thinking, I find myself.

'I EXIST ... BUT WHAT, THEN, AM I?' (Meditation 2)

Well, before undertaking this process of doubt what did I used to think I was?

1) A MAN, i.e., a rational animal. But Descartes has no time for definitions and dictionaries only for 'what [comes] into my thoughts spontaneously and quite naturally.' And that was:

2) that I had a BODY. But (says Descartes) a dead body has the same mechanical structure as a living one.

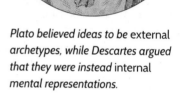

3) that I was nourished, self-moving, perceiving, thinking, all of which actions seem to me foreign to the body as such. I attributed them to the soul. (Descartes is citing Aristotle, who thinks of psyche

Plato believed ideas to be external archetypes, while Descartes argued that they were instead internal mental representations.

(soul) as a life-principle that varies in complexity. Cumulatively ranged along the hierarchy of soul-stages are plants (self-feeding), lower animals (self-feeding and self-moving), animals (the other two, plus perceiving), with humans (all three soul-capacities, plus that of thinking) at the top.)

4) And the soul? I didn't think about what it was like, but vaguely imagined it to be something ethereal and tenuous (wind, fire, ether) permeating my body.

Until I prove that I have a body, the first three Aristotelian capacities could be 'mere fabrications'. Therefore they are not essentially me. And even if I did have those capacities, sense-perception can be deceptive. What can I not doubt to be intrinsic to me? THINKING? Yes, that is inseparable from me (it was by thinking that I found myself to exist). It would be silly to use my imagination to get to know more clearly what I am – rather like saying: I can some see some truth now I'm awake, so

I'll go to sleep to see more. Therefore, instead of postulating spectral ethereal qualities, which are just distractions, I can know that what I essentially am is a thinking thing that has ideas.

IDEAS (ESPECIALLY MEDITATIONS 3 AND 4)

'Idea' is a term used by 17th- and 18th-century philosophers. The term is borrowed from Plato; and Descartes is largely responsible for modifying it.

An Idea, for Plato, was an objective external archetype (Table, Man, Beauty) by virtue of which each of the particular things that we call tables, men, beautiful *is* what it (imperfectly) is. The only certain knowledge we have is of Ideas (nowadays called 'Forms'); we only have *beliefs* about the things we sensorily experience.

Descartes turns Plato on his head. He makes an 'idea' a transient subjective mental representation rather than an eternal objectivity. What now count as ideas can be concepts, memories, imaginings, any part of my train of thought, and – an important new philosophical departure – that includes sensory perceptions and sensations in so far as they are experiences. Descartes' ideas are still the most certain items of knowledge, as were Plato's, but only because they are the entire sum of what we know. We can never get outside them.

Ideas (in Descartes' classification) are:

1) Innate (for example, mathematical concepts, and the idea of God, which 'I find in the storehouse of my mind');

2) Imaginary (I invent and summon them up at will);

3) Adventitious (ideas that simply occur, often as if caused by something outside me).

Whether or not any of these ideas are true, or (in the case of perceptions) correspond to reality, is a further question, but at any rate they 'cannot be called nothing', even if what they purport to represent is false or unreal.

Solipsism?

By the Third Meditation, then, Descartes has established that he exists. He has also discovered the criterion for truth, and the method of achieving knowledge (actually he has already reported this discovery in *The Discourse*): by strictly scanning his ideas and only endorsing those that are 'clear and distinct,' he has managed triumphantly to pull the rabbit of his own existence out of his cogitations' hat. But how can he prove the existence of anything else – anything outside himself and the ideas he is having?

'I certainly *seem* to see, to hear, to be warmed'. Indeed these sensory perceptions (ideas) of light, crackling and heat occur 'quite without my

CARTESIAN CIRCLE

In the Second and Fourth Objections, Descartes was criticized for 'arguing in a circle' – assuming in advance what he was setting out to prove. He seems to require God as guarantor of his clear and distinct ideas, yet already to have required clear and distinct ideas in order to prove God's existence.

Descartes' response was that clear and distinct ideas were ample guarantors, even without God, but that before God guaranteed them, their clarity and distinctness depended on their being looked at in the light of reason each time they were appealed to. Once God had been established by their means, it was no longer necessary, in the course of reasoning, to constantly unroll the certainties they had established and subject them once again to the natural light of reason. Having been guaranteed by what *they* had guaranteed (God), clear and distinct ideas could be used as rolled-up reliable steps in any argument.

consent' and prompt Descartes to believe that there is a fire in front of him. Yet this 'spontaneous impulse' is not self-guaranteeing. Only clear and distinct ideas authorized by the natural light of reason are undoubtable. How can he be sure that his subjective ideas of a fire actually correspond to a real fire objectively 'outside the mind'? What leverage can pry him loose from the closed circle of himself and his ideas (experiences)? The belief that I and my experiences are indeed all that exists is called 'solipsism'; Descartes is only inadvertently and temporarily solipsistic.

God (Meditations 3 and 5)

Until I know whether God exists, says Descartes, I can't be certain of anything else.

1) Descartes' causal argument for God's existence

The idea of God is one of the ideas that I find within myself. If true or accurate, an idea must be caused by what it represents, and it cannot be greater or more perfect than its cause (Descartes is falling back on an appalling Scholastic argument). The idea of God is too great to have been originated by me. It can't be false because it is so utterly clear and distinct, and can't be an amalgamation of ideas of perfection because it includes ideas of unity, simplicity, inseparability. It must in fact be the Craftsman's 'trademark' stamped on His work (like 'Nike' on your trainers), and innate.

2) Descartes' version of Anselm's Ontological Argument

I have an idea of God, just as I have ideas of triangles and mountains. It is possible, of course, that nothing Divine, triangular or mountainous exists outside my thoughts. However, if a triangle does exist, it has, by definition, three sides; if a mountain exists, it will be essentially flanked by a valley; if God exists, He must be a perfect being (when I think of Him, I necessarily attribute all perfections to Him, even if not specifying them individually). It is possible for either a triangle or mountain to exist as an idea without being instantiated in the world, but how could a being be perfect if it didn't exist?

God's existence is implied in His very essence. Unlike any other idea – except the idea of me – the idea of God necessitates that its content must exist. As with the cogito, to think about God guarantees His existence.

Argument for existence of material things (Meditation 6)

I often have adventitious ideas as if of material things outside my mind. Those that occur 'without my cooperation and often even against my will' (now, for instance, 'I feel the heat whether I want to or not'), cannot be caused by me. They must therefore be caused either by (genuinely existing) material things or by God. Descartes has 'proved' that his innate idea of God corresponds to God; and, because God is not a deceiver, can be certain that many of his passively received ideas not only seem, but *are*, caused by material things.

How we perceive material things (Meditations 2 and 6)

Descartes' argument for the external world only occurs in the Sixth and last Meditation. Already in the Second he shows that the world he will usher back in will not be the same as before he doubted it. 'Consider this piece of wax,' he says. It still tastes of the bee's honey, smells of the flowers it was gathered from, is white, hard, cold; if struck, it makes a faint sound. Leave it by the fire, however, and it loses that residual taste and smell, and its shape, size and colour change. It becomes liquid and hot, difficult to touch, and no longer emitting any sound if struck. All of its previous features have altered, 'yet the wax remains'. What is the wax, then? Not the properties that I observe by means of the senses, since these are subject to change – to so many permutations that I'm unable to run through all of them in my imagination. No, ultimately, the wax is an extended, flexible, changeable thing. It must be by 'purely mental scrutiny' that I perceive the wax (this particular piece, and, still more, wax in general).

I have free will, and it is my responsibility to *assent* (or not) to appearances. I have to judge, in each case, whether or not my ideas actually *resemble* the true nature of the things that cause them. Thus, after using my judgement properly, I find that I have two different ideas of the sun. One, acquired from the senses, presents it as a small, round, yellow disk; the other, based on astronomical and mathematical reasoning, shows it to be considerably larger than the earth. (Also, of

PERCEPTION AND JUDGEMENT

I might say that, when I look out of the window, I see men walking in the street. What I in fact see – before bringing my judgement into play – is a whole set of hats and cloaks, which could conceivably be concealing artificial machines operated by springs. 'I *judge* that they are men'.

You might object that, had the men been naked, rather than hatted and cloaked, reason would not have been required to deduce that they were men. Descartes' point, however, is that perception always requires judgement. Any animal could perceive what I first perceived. Only a freely judging human mind can distinguish the wax from its exterior forms, or the men from their accoutrements. Even physical things are 'perceived ... by the intellect alone'. Back to clear and distinct ideas.

course – although Descartes can't say so – this idea would reveal the sun to be motionless, rather than rising in the east and setting in the west, as it seems to do). If we misperceive, he says, that is only because it is beneficial for us to do so. He admits that we are sometimes deceived by our senses detrimentally – the sufferer from dropsy, for instance, has an insatiable thirst, even though to drink is precisely what will worsen his condition – but how good God is that usually thirst is so helpful(!) As long as I use my judgement properly, I shall be fine.

A MATHEMATICAL WORLD, AND THE DISTINCTION BETWEEN PRIMARY AND SECONDARY QUALITIES

The wax example establishes a new idea of what it is to perceive, and simultaneously a new idea of the nature of the world. Like Galileo and other scientists of the time, Descartes realizes that the world is not as we perceive it – that our perceptions, rather than mirroring things outside us, are the result of our sensory organs interacting with phenomena such as light waves, sound waves, texture and chemicals. When he

Like Galileo, Descartes understood that the world was not entirely as we perceived it.

sets out to 'distinguish the wax from its outward forms – take the clothes off, as it were', what he is left with is just (the idea of) something three-dimensionally extended in space, an underlying geometrical structure. He concludes that the fundamental property of matter is 'extension'. In itself, the unsensed world is colourless, soundless, tasteless, odourless, textureless.

Our senses rarely 'show us what external bodies are like in themselves', writes Descartes in *Principles of Philosophy*. 'We have every reason to conclude that the properties in external objects to which we apply the terms light, colour, smell, taste, sound, heat and cold [are] simply various dispositions in those objects which make them able to set up various kinds of motions in our nerves'. Nor are we 'entitled to say that anything reaches the brain except for the local motion of the nerves themselves'. The sensation of hardness, for instance, simply tells us that the 'hard' thing resists our hands. Descartes has made a crucial distinction between what Locke would later call primary and secondary qualities (see p.60).

Using our clear and distinct ideas, however, we have access to the measurable, quantifiable world, and to a God-like knowledge of the reality beyond the 'obscure and confused ideas' we have of it via our sensory perceptions. Extended material things belong to 'the subject-matter of pure mathematics', and must possess all the qualities (shape, size, weight, number, movement or stillness) that we clearly and distinctly understand.

ME – MIND/BODY OR INTERMINGLED

If colours, tastes, smells, sounds aren't in the stark objective world, there has to be a subjectivity outside that world to glean them from it – a mind to which the appearances appear, even while it reasons that they do not (as such) correspond to reality. It was because he was so ardently scientific, a proponent of what was then called 'the mechanical philosophy', that Descartes needed to postulate a separate 'I' which was capable of (mis) perceiving, and of having free will. But he didn't originate the distinction between mental and physical, mind and body. Centuries earlier Plato had transformed the life-force *psyche* into the reasoning, immortal essence that makes us human and that puts us at odds with the natural world. The early Christian Church, and then Augustine in the fourth century, developed this concept of soul.

There is some scholarly controversy over whether Descartes, who claims to use the terms 'mind' and 'soul' interchangeably, in fact employs them differently ('mind' being sometimes preferable because more scientific-sounding). At any rate he argues that 'I' (mind or soul) must necessarily be 'distinct and separable from my body', since what I clearly and distinctly understand can be made by God just as I understand it, and I understand myself separately from the 'extended, non-thinking thing' that I needed to prove, and to which I am connected.

Yet Descartes needs the 'I' to be part of, as well as other than, the causally-determined world. After all, mental events cause physical ones, and vice versa. My desire for a cake causes me to reach across the table; burning my hand causes me pain. During his dissections, Descartes noticed that the pineal gland lacked a symmetrical double (unlike brain hemispheres, lungs, kidneys, and so on). He claims that 'although the soul is joined to the whole body, nevertheless . . . it exercises its functions more particularly [in the pineal gland] than in all the others'; and he invokes the spurious 'animal spirits' as a mechanism.

Descartes also acknowledges that 'I am not merely present in my body as a sailor is present in a ship, but … intermingled with it, so that I and the body form a unit.' If I were not, I would simply deduce that damage has been done to me in the way a sailor may deduce that there is a rent in the side of his ship when he sees it listing in the water (apparently what happened when the Titanic hit the iceberg). As it is, I

When the Titanic hit the iceberg, passengers deduced *that it had been damaged – but when our body is injured, we* feel *the damage directly.*

don't *infer* that I have been stabbed in the leg from observing a flow of blood. Rather, I *feel* the stab – instantly and from the inside. (It is hard to square Descartes' acknowledgement of our hybrid nature with his view that mind and body are distinct, as Princess Elisabeth of Bohemia pointed out.)

WHERE THE MEDITATIONS LEAVES US

This whole thought experiment is a return to first principles, spurning 'preconceived opinions', his own and anyone else's. But it is also the reader's thought experiment. Descartes is not so much elevating himself as elevating every-I. 'What we properly call "good sense" or "reason"', he declared in the *Discourse*, 'is naturally equal in all men'. So much for Plato's philosopher-kings! Not that Descartes is saying that everyone is equally intelligent or that all opinions are equally valid – the 'good sense' needs to be properly applied; mere 'conjecture' is inadequate. But if we make sure to accept as true only 'what we can clearly and evidently intuit or deduce', then, using the 'natural light of reason', we can follow 'long chains composed of very simple and easy reasonings', much as geometers do, and ultimately arrive at truths about the world.

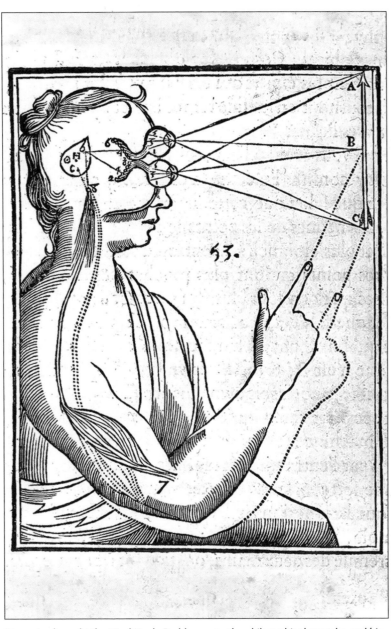

Descartes brought the Mind/Body Problem onto the philosophical agenda, and his dualist position is the intractable common sense fallback as alternatives fail.

Descartes has established a new basis and arbitrator for philosophical enquiry – the thinking individual who moves outwards from the ideas he indubitably has to truth/knowledge that is objectively certain.

THINKING EXTENDED, WORLD DIMINISHED

What Descartes gives with one hand he takes away with the other. He has extended the boundaries of what counts as thought from purely rational activity to any form of consciousness. For him, and for us ever afterwards, thinking includes doubting, asserting, imagining and willing, and also having sensations (pain, for instance) and sensory perceptions. (The seems-to-me part of sense-perception, 'is simply thinking', he says.)

But the self is now subjective, immaterial, somehow outside physical stuff, even its own body. And, even though it turns out to be true – in one way – that I really *am* seeing the firelight, hearing flame-crackling, feeling warm, yet in another way my perceptions remain (even after he has 'proved' the external world) a sort of delusion. They do not accurately represent the real colourless, soundless, odourless, tasteless, un-temperatured things outside my mind. Colours, sounds, smells, tastes, feeling hot or cold, are merely the interaction between certain sorts of atomic structures and our senses. The self, endowed with free will and marooned in consciousness, is exiled from the mechanical, causally determined world. Science since Descartes has made this world yet more austere, so much so that ironically the mind, which Descartes claimed to be indubitable, has itself become dubious.

How – or if – physical reality can accommodate the mental is the question currently topping the philosophical agenda; and this *Mind/ Body Problem* is often and unfairly blamed on Descartes. In any case, he has the last word. For all the attempts to squash the 'I' back down into the natural world, Cartesian dualism remains the default position, even if not acknowledged as such. The mind-denying philosophers keep inadvertently tumbling back into it.

Key points

- Descartes repudiated Scholasticism, and the authority of scripture and Aristotle. He sought to find 'the first causes and the true principles which enable us to deduce the reasons for everything we are capable of knowing'.

- In his own time, he was renowned as a great scientist, as well as a great philosopher. He introduced the view of the world that we still have as mathematically measurable and ultimately explicable by science.

- *The Meditations* goes through three stages of doubt; till:
  a) Scepticism culminates in the Cogito ('I think, I am')

  b) What then am I? – a mental substance which has ideas, some of which suggest that there is an external world (to which they correspond).

  c) Clear and distinct ideas are the criterion for ascertaining truth.

  d) God's existence is 'proved' by means of the Causal and Ontological Arguments.

  e) Cartesian Circle – does Descartes use clear and distinct ideas to 'prove' God's existence, which in turn 'proves' the validity of the clear and distinct ideas?

f) Argument for the external world. Some of his ideas occur whether he wants them to or not. Now that he has proved the existence of an undeceiving God, he knows that, as long as he conscientiously applies reason, he can ascertain which are accurate.

g) Perception involves reasoning.

h) Reason tells us that the qualities of size, shape, bulk, number, movement or stillness are as they seem, but that colours, sounds, tastes and smells are not. Descartes was making a distinction between primary and secondary qualities (without using those terms).

i) Descartes' 'mechanical philosophy' has given us our bleak world-view in which, essentially, physics is the ultimate determinant of truth.

j) How dualistic was Descartes? He argues that each human is a mental substance somehow attached to, and operating, a physical substance, but also states that the mental is 'intermingled' with the physical.

k) Still, he leaves the 'hard problem' of how the mental interacts with the physical (or is, in fact, anything other than physical).

Chapter 3

John Locke (1632–1704)

Even in his own time, Locke had an international reputation. He was admired in France and America especially, and the French *philosophe* Voltaire dubbed him 'the Hercules of metaphysics'. He is often considered the founder of empiricism, although Francis Bacon and Thomas Hobbes had already also grounded their thought in sensory experience. Like Descartes (who influenced him), he advocated the pursuit of scientific discovery untrammelled by religious texts or clerics, but, whereas Descartes' aim had been to rebuild the entire edifice of what we know, Locke's was the more modest one of 'clearing the ground a little,

John Locke had an international reputation even in his own time.

and removing some of the rubbish that lies in the way to knowledge'. He himself produced no science.

Like many other Enlightenment thinkers, Locke was deeply involved with the political affairs of his time. His political theories probably influenced the American revolt against English colonialism and the writing of the Declaration of Independence. He is called 'the father of liberalism' for promoting the view that government was for the sake of the governed, and that we have inalienable rights to life, freedom and property, but he has inspired rightwing free-market libertarianism as well as more benign traditional liberalism.

Life

John Locke was born in 1632 in Somerset into a Puritan family. His father, a legal clerk, fought on the Parliamentarian side in the English Civil War. Thanks to a rich patron, Locke was sent to the best school in England, Westminster, and won a scholarship to Christ Church College, Oxford, where he was exasperated by Aristotelian scholasticism and ended up studying medicine. While tutoring, he became part of a group of pioneering 'natural philosophers' (the 17th century term for scientists), and shared an experimental laboratory. By luck, he was delegated to deliver medicinal water to a visiting dignitary, Lord Ashley, and soon afterwards Locke moved to Ashley's London house and became his secretary, tutor to his son, doctor, and close advisor, all the closer after conducting the delicate liver operation that saved Ashley's life.

In 1668 Locke was elected to join the newly formed Royal Society (his friends Isaac Newton and Robert Boyle were key members), which was dedicated to 'improving natural knowledge' and had the typically Enlightenment motto 'Nullius in Verba' – take no-one's word for it. It was more informal meetings with friends that inspired Locke to begin the *Essay Concerning Human Understanding* in 1671. Thanks to Ashley, Locke became Secretary of the Board of Trade and Plantations, was involved in England's financial organisation, and almost certainly helped draft the constitution of the state of Carolina. Between 1675 and 1678, he lived in France, where he met Descartes' followers.

In 1682, Ashley (by now first Earl of Shaftesbury) was in disgrace for having opposed the succession of Charles II's Catholic brother to the throne. Locke found it prudent to flee to Holland where, due to his terror of assassination by English spies, he adopted the name Doctor van der Linden. Only in 1689, after the Glorious Revolution had ousted James II, did he return to England – in the royal yacht with the future queen, Mary.

Throughout his travels and his various appointments, Locke had been writing on philosophy, economics, education and theology (as he continued doing till death), and finishing his two most famous works – the *Essay Concerning Human Understanding* and *Two Treatises of Government* – which were published in 1689. The latter was anonymous, as was the *Letter on Toleration*, published the following year, and both proved contentious. He sometimes praised the unknown author but would become hysterical if even his closest friends suggested it was him, only acknowledging authorship in his will.

The new King William offered Locke various posts, including that of ambassador, but he opted for the less onerous Board of Trade. Severely asthmatic, he spent the last years of his life in the Essex home of Sir Francis and Lady Masham. An old, once-amorous, friend, she was reading him the Psalms as he died.

Robert Boyle was a friend of John Locke and a fellow member of the Royal Society.

ESSAY CONCERNING HUMAN UNDERSTANDING

Locke sought to discover and delineate the way we perceive, think and use language, and how far what we perceive, think and say amounts to knowing.

'I suspected we began at the wrong end', he says (in the introductory first chapter), when we assume that we can 'let loose our thoughts into the vast ocean of *Being*, as if all that boundless extent were the natural and undoubted possession of our understandings'. We should first 'examine our own powers and see to what things they were adapted.'

No Innate Ideas

Like Descartes, Locke thinks that the mind has 'no other immediate object but its own ideas, which it alone does or can contemplate', and that ideas are the building blocks of knowledge. There is, however, an ambiguity in what Locke means by 'idea'. In saying that it is 'whatsoever is the object of the understanding when a man thinks … or whatever it is which the mind can be employed about in thinking', does he mean that an idea is a static mental image (caused, in the case of sense-perception, by things outside the mind), or does he mean that it is the *action* of perceiving or thinking? Either way (and philosophers argue for each), 'the mind … stirs not one jot beyond those ideas which sense or reflection have offered for its contemplation'.

The short first book of the *Essay* is devoted to repudiating the theory (held by Descartes and other rationalists) that children are born with certain logical, metaphysical and moral ideas already imprinted by God on their souls. Innate ideas can be invoked to place specified religious, moral and political ideas beyond criticism. It was certainly convenient for Descartes to 'find' the idea of God in 'the storehouse of [his] mind' since the very idea of God seemed to guarantee God's existence, which in turn could guarantee the veracity of Descartes' other ideas.

Locke argues that even if everyone everywhere had a notion of God, it would not thereby follow that the idea of God was innate, and that anyway 'history tells us the contrary'. Some societies have many gods, others have none, and the word 'god', translatable across languages, conveys 'contrary and inconsistent ideas and conceptions of him'. Children aren't born knowing about God; and, rather than considering a child's idea of God to be the mark of His workmanship (as Descartes does), it is surely more sensible to regard that idea as the mark of the child's teacher.

Similarly, anyone who has 'looked abroad beyond the smoke of their own chimneys' can find no universally accepted principles. Moral rules differ in different societies. And the fact that people so easily, often, and 'with allowance', abandon the morality they profess is 'a proof that it is not innate'. Virtue is approved of, not because it is innate but because it is 'profitable'.

Locke also dismisses the notion that logic is innate. The only way it could be known whether infants have innate ideas would be if infants showed evidence of believing these ideas. But there is none. Locke anticipates the rationalist retort – that children will assent to the laws of logic, for instance 'when they come to the use of reason'. But that, he replies, is effectively to say that children 'know and know them not at the same time'. In any case, logical rules are unknown not only by children but by 'idiots, savages, and illiterate people, being of all others the least corrupted by custom or borrowed opinions'. Even the law of identity is not universal, different societies having different ideas of what it is to be identical. Pythagoras, for instance, believed we are the same man if we are the same soul. [But, *pace* Locke, might we not all share the same concept of 'same', and simply *apply* it differently?]

Thus, 'To ask at what time a man has first any ideas is to ask when he begins to perceive: having ideas and perception being the same thing.'

Tabula rasa

Having debunked the theory of innate ideas, Locke urges us: 'Let us then suppose the mind to be, as we say, white paper void of all characters, without any ideas. How comes it to be furnished? Whence comes it by that vast store which the busy and boundless fancy of man has painted on it with an almost endless variety? Whence has it all the materials of reason and knowledge? To this I answer, in one word, from *experience*; in that all our knowledge is founded, and from that it ultimately derives itself.' We begin to have ideas as soon as we begin to perceive, he says, 'having ideas and perception being the same thing'.

Sensation plus reflection give rise to knowledge

Locke argues that sensations alone would be insufficient to give us knowledge. The senses 'let in' ideas to 'the dark room' of the mind, but the mind is 'merely passive' in receiving these ideas. It is active in 'reflecting on its own operations' on the ideas it has received. By this sort of internal perception, ideas are stored in the memory, named, compared, combined and generalized.

Knowledge is 'the perception of the connexion and agreement, or disagreement and repugnancy, of any of our ideas'. We perceive the identity or diversity of ideas, their relations, their co-existence (that iron has magnetic properties, for instance), and their correspondence to real things. This fourth type of perception is, however, problematic for Locke, for if ideas (whether these are processes or internal objects) are subjective, and are the sum total of our experience, how can we get outside them to see if they correspond to the qualities or things that cause them? A portrait can only be known to be a good likeness if you have seen the sitter as well as the portrait of her.

The mind, says Locke, for all its wanderings above the clouds, 'stirs not one jot beyond those ideas which sense or reflection have offered for its contemplation'. We are, then, forever shut into our minds (or perhaps into the ideas in our minds), and excluded from the external world, except in so far as echoes and rumours of it reach us through the senses' windows. However, since our simple ideas of primary qualities (see p.60) are directly caused by, and exactly resemble, some of the qualities outside us, perhaps we have what the mystical poet William Blake called 'chinks on our cavern' – some revealing inlets from the external world.

> 'External and internal sensation are the only passages that I can find of knowledge to the understanding. These alone, as far as I can discover, are the windows by which light is let into this *dark room*. For, methinks, the *understanding* is not much unlike a closet wholly shut from light, with only some little opening left, to let in external visible resemblances, or *ideas* of things without [outside].' John Locke
>
> 'How do you know but every bird that cuts the airy way, is an immense world of delight, closed by your senses five?' William Blake

ARGUMENTS FOR LOCKE'S REPRESENTATIVE THEORY OF PERCEPTION

The sort of mistakes in perceiving that inspire scepticism about the existence of the external world can instead serve as the thin end of the wedge for the theory that we only perceive things indirectly – that what we perceive are not things themselves but the ideas (called 'sense data' since the 20th century) that are caused by the qualities of things.

1) The argument from illusion

Our senses sometimes mislead us – a stick looks bent in water; a mirage convinces the wanderer in the desert that they see an oasis. Therefore, whether we are looking at a stick that is genuinely bent or at a stick in water; at a real oasis or a mirage, we have the *same* visual impression. What we *actually* see is our own internal visual image, which in one case corresponds to what is actually in front of us and in the other does not.

2) The argument from the relativity of perception

What I see when I look at a table or at a landscape will vary according to the angle or distance I view it from, the amount of light, and the soundness of my eyesight. Again, what I directly perceive is not the table or landscape but my own internal visual impressions, which have some sort of correspondence to what is 'out there' in the physical world.

3) The argument from physics

Galileo, Descartes and other 'natural philosophers' had come to realize that what we call 'sounds' are not outside us, but the product of vibrating soundwaves interacting with our auditory nerves and brain. Soon, too, it would be understood that colour is not inherent in objects but is a matter of the impact of light waves on our retinas and optic nerves. Plenty of other creatures lack the visual equipment with which to extrapolate colour from light-waves. So our impressions of sounds and colours do not echo or mirror anything in the external world, rather they are produced by oscillations outside us stimulating our sense organs.

4) The time-lag argument

This is a modern addition to Locke's arguments. The sun's light takes eight minutes to reach us, so the sun we see is actually the sun of eight minutes ago; if the sun exploded, we would continue to 'see' it eight minutes after it had in fact ceased to exist. Recently, a star's 'explosion' was observed that had really happened in Elizabeth I's reign, more than 500 years ago. Similarly, although thunder and lightning are simultaneous, thunder seems to occur later than lightning because sound waves take longer to reach us and we see the lightning-flash first.

Therefore, what we immediately experience by sight, touch, hearing and so forth are the ideas (sense data) caused by physical objects (and their qualities) in the external world. Ideas (sense data) of qualities may resemble qualities, or, in the case of colours, sounds, and so forth, be the result of the qualities' impact on our sense organs. Like Descartes, Locke gives us an account of the world that consists of measurable, countable extended things. This physicist account includes light waves, which interact with optic nerves and cause us to have the experience of colour; and vibrations which, in conjunction with our auditory equipment, cause us to hear sounds. If all creatures with sense-organs and consciousness were removed from the world, there would continue to be light-waves but there would be no colour; there would be pulsations in the air, but no longer any experienced sounds; particles would increase or decrease their speed of movement, but no one would feel hot or cold; and so on.

MENTAL FURNITURE
1) Simple ideas
Simple ideas are the basic building blocks of all our knowledge: the mind can construct complex ideas out of the simple ideas it has received, but cannot invent or construct new simple ideas. Many simple ideas (such as those of smells and tastes) only reach us through one sense, and have no specific name.

We have simple ideas of **primary and secondary qualities**. Primary qualities are the shape, size, weight and number of an object, and whether it is in motion or at rest. These qualities are in the object whether we perceive it or not (i.e., exist independent of our perception), and remain in it despite alterations (if you divide and subdivide a grain of wheat, it still has size and stillness).

Primary qualities are mathematically measurable, and are available to two senses – sight and touch. The ideas we have of primary qualities resemble the qualities themselves. We can be mistaken as to the actual intrinsic shape, but not about the object's having a shape.

Secondary qualities 'are nothing in the objects themselves but powers to produce various sensations in us'. Locke is following the contemporary science. Sound waves had been discovered in the 16th century, and, along with the realization that sound is a matter of vibrations making an impact upon our auditory nerves, it was becoming apparent that colour, temperature, smells and tastes are also not intrinsically the way they seem. Secondary qualities in themselves, says Locke, are nothing like what we perceive; without anyone to perceive them they 'are reduced to their causes'. But is he entitled to say this? According to his empiricist theory, all that we perceive are

The Human Condition by René Magritte © ADAGP, Paris and DACS, London 2018
Belgian surrealist artist Magritte wrote of this painting, 'In front of a window
seen from inside a room, I placed a painting representing exactly that part of
the landscape that was hidden from view by the painting. Therefore, the tree
represented in the painting hid from view the tree situated behind it, outside the
room. It existed for the spectator, as it were, simultaneously in his mind, as both
inside the room in the painting, and outside in the real landscape. Which is how we
see the world: we see it as being outside ourselves even though it is only a mental
representation of it that we experience inside ourselves.'

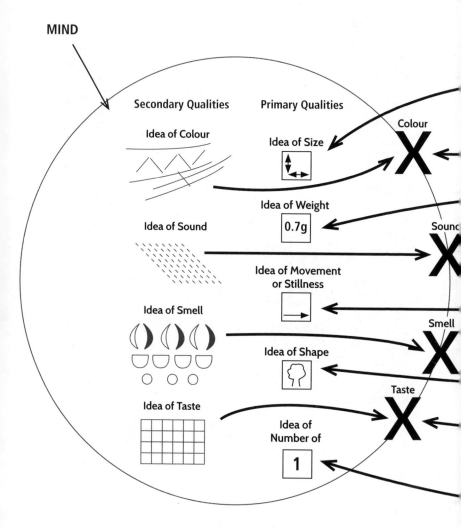

EXTERNAL WORLD

PHYSICAL SUBSTANCE

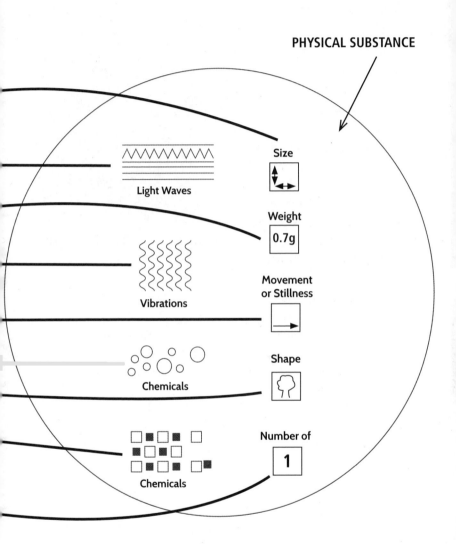

Primary qualities directly cause ideas that resemble them.

Secondary qualities interact with the sense organs, nerves and brain to produce ideas that do not resemble, but systematically correspond to, them.

THE MOLYNEUX PROBLEM

The Irish scientist William Molyneux wrote to Locke, posing a question germane to the theory of simple ideas. Suppose someone blind from birth, who had been taught to distinguish cubes and spheres by touch, were suddenly able to see – would he be able to tell by sight alone which shape was which? No, was Locke's answer. Given that the mind is a blank slate at birth, and only accumulates simple ideas through experience, there is no reason for it automatically to relate simple tactile ideas to simple visual ideas.

William Molyneux asked whether a blind man, suddenly granted sight, would be able to tell one shape from another.

ideas, and our knowledge (which consists of comparing, compounding and abstracting our ideas) does not extend beyond them: so how can we know that qualities that we don't perceive are dissimilar to our perceptions of them?

Locke also mentions a tertiary quality – the power by one object to produce change in the primary qualities of another object so that the latter acts on our senses differently from the way it initially did (for example, the way fire melts wax and alters its colour). According to Locke, it is from our experience of willing parts of our bodies to move that we ascribe 'active' and 'passive power' not just to ourselves but to animals, water, fire and so forth when they move or change the things around them.

2) Complex ideas

These are made by the mind out of simple ones, and are of three sorts:

i) Mode: the attribute of a thing (triangularity), the way things are arranged (a line), the way something is regarded (beauty, theft).

ii) Substance: 'a collection of a certain number of simple ideas, considered as united in one thing' – equating to a self-subsistent entity (a man) or a collection of entities (an army).

iii) Relation: ideas of reciprocal relation or comparison (father and son, bigger and less, cause and effect).

3) Substance

Since Aristotle, metaphysicians had regarded any independently-existing thing as a **'substance'** which persists through time while its qualities, modes and so on change. Similarly, Locke says that we not only form complex ideas as a result of experiencing the regular co-existence of particular qualities, but that the qualities' co-existence is 'supposed to flow from [some] particular internal constitution of unknown essence'. But does he think that *supposition* justified? He mentions the absurdity of an intelligent Catholic being prepared to 'swallow' – against the clear evidence of his senses – the doctrine of Transubstantiation, which claims that when the priest at Mass says certain words, the *substance* of the bread he is holding becomes Christ, while its *qualities* remain those of bread. And he sometimes implies that any notion of substance is similarly unwarranted. According to his Indirect Realism, it is only 'the particular qualities' that we have clear ideas of. How, then, are we entitled to postulate that there is anything underlying them? Often he seems to dismiss the notion of **'pure substance in general'** as an imaginary stopgap, like the one he ascribes to an Indian philosopher trying to explain what supports the world in space (an elephant standing on a tortoise standing on 'something, he knew not what').

Yet doesn't his theory require that **'a particular substance'** underlies each co-existing set of primary and secondary qualities? In response to criticism from the Protestant Bishop of Worcester, Locke insists that he has not 'discarded' substance, it is just that we have only 'a very imperfect, obscure, inadequate idea' of it. Perhaps that assertion is purely politic; it is debatable whether Locke is being sceptical (or ironical) about 'substance'; whether he is critiquing, or simply reporting on, the ordinary meaning of the term; or whether he does indeed think that there is 'substance in general', and/ or that primary and secondary qualities are underpinned and integrated by 'particular sorts of substances' (his theory seems to require this) – whether, perhaps, he even identifies particular substance with 'real essence'.

4) Abstract ideas

i) 'The mind makes the particular ideas received from particular objects to become general' by extrapolating such ideas from the actual concrete experience of them and considering them separately, then naming them. Observing the same colour in chalk, snow and milk, we call it 'whiteness'.

ii) Also, (having assumed that each co-occurring group of qualities is underpinned by a 'particular substance'), we generalise from the recurrent similarity of 'particular substances' to the idea of some 'general substance' ('man', 'tiger', 'tulip', 'gold'). But are we justified in doing this?

5) Nominal and real essence

Locke says that the classification of species is just man-made, 'the workmanship of the understanding', nothing but the arbitrary construction of abstract ideas, so that a genus or species is not a natural kind, and has merely a 'nominal essence'. On the other hand, he speaks of 'the real internal, but generally (in substances) unknown, constitution of things, whereon their discoverable qualities depend [which] may be called their essence'. When he alludes to 'the supposed real essences of substances', that 'supposed' is typically prevaricating. Does he mean that we are wrong to believe that there are substances, and that they have real essences? Or does he mean that there are indeed real essences to objects, even if we can only conjecture what these essences are?

Locke adopts his friend Robert Boyle's atomic (or 'corpuscular') theory, although he provides no arguments or empirical justification for doing so. He says that our ideas of secondary qualities are nothing like the way those qualities really are. 'We may conceive', however (but does he mean that we *should* conceive?) that the ideas we have of them are produced 'by the operation of insensible particles on our senses'. Just as microscopes reveal more to us than the naked eye can do, so, if God had given us more-than-microscopic eyes (He hasn't because we don't need them), we would be able to perceive secondary qualities as the minuscule primary qualities that they really are.

Perhaps, then, Locke thinks that qualities 'inhere' in objects, and that objects do have real essences, which are atomic combinations – structures that we can never have ideas of, but that nonetheless can rightly be postulated to exist. Perhaps it may even be the case that sometimes the 'nominal essence' which our abstract idea has constructed actually coincides with its unknown, unknowable real essence. Could he mean that an object's 'real essence' is its substance? If so, is a substance simply the unqualitied 'support' of qualities, or does it have qualities itself?

LANGUAGE

Locke sees language as being mainly concerned with naming. Just as he thinks that what we directly perceive are ideas (caused by the things we only indirectly perceive), so he thinks that words stand for the ideas we have of things, and not directly for the things themselves. Words serve as 'outward marks of our internal ideas'. Constant usage sets up a connexion between certain sounds and the ideas they stand for, so that they excite similar ideas in speaker and listener. This is of course hugely problematic, and would later be contested by Wittgenstein and others, as would Locke's starting assumption that language is mainly concerned with naming.

He maintains that only particular things exist, and that we make 'general ideas' for which we have 'general words.' (See Abstract Ideas, p. 66)

PERSONAL IDENTITY

What is it to be a person at a particular time? What is it to be a person over time? Can something change and yet remain the same – and the same what? Locke argues that something can be the same x without being the same y. His treatment of personal identity, totally original then, is still the canonical starting-point in discussing this question, and he set the fashion for thought puzzles.

THE LIMITS OF KNOWLEDGE

'[O]ur faculties are not fitted to penetrate into the internal fabric and real essences of bodies,' wrote Locke. It could be said that his pessimism has since been invalidated, for much of the inner workings and atomic structure that he considered unknowable has apparently been revealed. But *only* apparently. The whole scientific enterprise is conducted in a Lockean spirit. Any scientific theory is merely provisional. The concepts used in science, and conclusions reached, are taken as temporary, constrained by the way, and extent to which, we can observe and measure.

He begins by saying that non-living things become different entities simply by losing or gaining particles, whereas for machines and for living things what matters is the 'continued organization' of the whole. In the case of machines, repairing, adding or subtracting parts enables them to continue functioning as 'the same organized body', and this addition is done from outside. With living things, the change comes from within (acorns become oaks, colts develop into full-grown horses). But whether we can correctly call something that changes the same (over time) depends on how we classify it. In line with his theory that it is ideas we perceive, and ideas (not things) that we name, he distinguishes between something being the same man, the same soul, the same substance and the same person. He argues that, these concepts (where instantiated in the external world) don't necessarily coincide or dovetail.

The idea of 'man', says Locke, is not that of 'thinking being', but is 'nothing else but of an animal of such a certain form'. If the soul of Heliogabalus (a wicked Roman emperor) were reincarnated as a hog, we wouldn't say the hog was the same man, or the same physical substance as Heliogabalus. But would that soul be the same person as Heliogabalus? After all, the soul is a mental substance.

No, says Locke. Despite protesting belief in substance to the Bishop of Worcester, he not only denies that mental substance (the soul) is what determines personal identity, he daringly queries the notion of mental substance itself – even mooting the possibility that God could have endowed some material things with the faculty of thinking. Just as 'animal identity' is preserved in identity of life, rather than of substance,

so personal identity is not constituted by physical or mental substance but by whatever enables a thinking intelligent being to 'consider itself as itself' in the present and 'in different times and places; which it does only by that consciousness which is inseparable from thinking and, as it seems to me, essential to it: it being impossible for anyone to perceive without perceiving that he does perceive'. What is crucial is *the act of considering*, not the *thing* which considers.

Locke is de-reifying (de-thing-izing) the Cartesian self, making it instead a process of consciousness that extends backwards in memory, and forwards in self-concern. If my little finger is cut off, that finger ceases to be me, but if 'this consciousness goes along with the little finger', I would in future be, not my body, but the severed little finger. The hog would be Heliogabalus if he remembered having been Heliogabalus. If the soul of a prince is swapped with the soul of a cobbler, then, as long the soul is 'carrying

If the soul of Heliogabalus was reincarnated as a hog, we would not say he was the same man, but would he be the same person?

with it the consciousness of the prince's past life', the erstwhile cobbler would not be the same *man* as the prince but would be the same *person*.

As well as conveying the idea of consciousness persisting over time, 'person' has a legal dimension. There could potentially be two persons in one body, or one person who alternates between bodies; and, if someone cannot remember what he does at night, then the 'day-man' should not in justice be punished for the 'night-man's' actions (they are different persons). Locke admits that such a plea could not be used as defence in a legal trial, due to the impossibility of proving it, but it will certainly work at the Last Judgement!

Criticisms of Locke on personal identity

1) As in his treatment of substance, Locke vacillates between making the way we ordinarily speak the deciding factor of identity, and querying our ordinary terms.

2) He may be assuming in advance what he needs to prove: Bishop Butler objected that to talk of memory/self-consciousness already presupposes a substance.

3) Locke unintentionally reifies consciousness, making it similar to a thinking substance.

4) Various critics have questioned the memory criterion. Locke's contemporary, Thomas Reid, imagines a naughty boy who is beaten for stealing apples; who a few years later is a brave lieutenant leading the troops and planting their flag on the conquered hill; and who eventually becomes a general. The lieutenant remembers being the naughty boy, and the general remembers being the brave lieutenant but cannot remember being the naughty boy. Is the general, then, not the same person as the boy, even though the lieutenant *is*? Shouldn't identity be transitive?

5) We often misremember. How accurate do memories need to be to count as memories at all?

LOCKE'S POLITICAL PHILOSOPHY

While studying at Oxford, Locke was morally and politically conservative, but he later became 'the father of liberalism' – its father, however, not its embodiment. Yet if today's readers of his political writings are disappointed that he is not as forward-looking as they might wish, that is because they are forgetting how revolutionary Locke was in his own time, and how much the sort of thinking he originated has developed since then.

In his *Essay on Toleration* (1667), and *Letter on Toleration* (anonymously published in 1689), he decried political or legal compulsion in matters of religion. What leads people to salvation is 'the inward constraints of [God's] spirit on their minds', rather than 'any forced exterior performance'. But Catholics – because they owed allegiance to the (foreign) Pope – and atheists – because they are 'wild beasts' and cannot be trusted – were exempt from toleration.

The first of Locke's *Two Treatises of Government* is a riposte to Robert Filmer's tract *Patriarcha*, which advocated the Divine Right of Kings. The second, outlining the origin, extent and aim of civil government, was, and remains, seminal in political philosophy.

Civil Government (Second Treatise)

Like Thomas Hobbes (1588–1679), Locke proposed a social contract theory, based on empirical facts about humans' habits and desires, but his 'facts', and therefore his theory, were more optimistic and lenient than his predecessor's, even though he too lived through turbulent times.

For Hobbes, the state of nature which humans avoid by making their contract, is the war of all against all, 'where every man is enemy to every man', and where the threat of violence outlaws industry, farming, transport, learning and culture. Everyone's life is 'solitary, poor, nasty, brutish, and short'. But the contract which enables us to avoid this 'state of war' is also grim. Each person must agree to surrender themselves to the absolute authority of one man, or one assembly of men: the great monster Leviathan. Hobbes does not endorse the Divine Right of Kings (Leviathan's power is derived from the people); but he considered monarchy the best form of government, and that not only a state's laws but also its morality are for its king to decide. So-called tyranny is merely 'monarchy misliked'.

In Locke's more benign state of nature, people are free, equal and independent. The law of nature enjoins us to respect one another's 'natural rights' to life, liberty and property, but, when disobeyed, it is hard to enforce. Hence the 'original compact' in which 'every man, by consenting with others to make one body politic under one government, puts himself under an obligation to every one of that society to submit

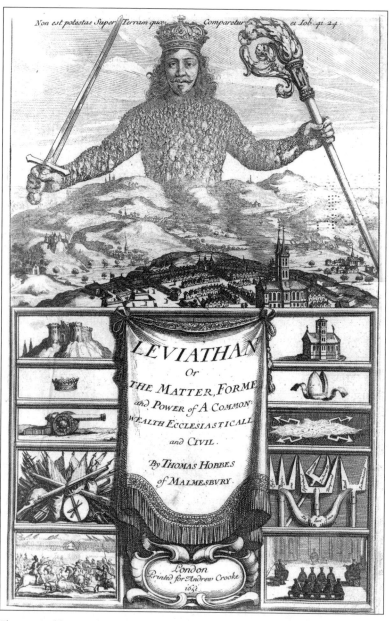

Thomas Hobbes put forward his case for a strong state in *Leviathan*, first published in 1651.

to the determination of the majority'. People show their tacit consent to obey the country's laws simply by walking along its highways.

For Locke, 'the end of government is the good of mankind' and the preservation of property and other natural rights. It is legitimate to try and unseat any government that fails to do this – Locke is extremely daring in offering such a licence for revolution.

Property

God gave the earth to everyone, but 'the labour of [a man's] body, and the work of his hands, we may say, are properly his.' Therefore, whatever he 'mixes his labour with' – tilling, planting, cultivating – rightfully becomes his exclusive property. After all, he has 'removed [it] from the common state nature hath placed it in'. It would otherwise remain as it is, be useless, and eventually decay. Each man is justified in amassing as much as will serve for his use without 'straitening' anybody else; he offends against the common law of nature if his fruits rot, his venison putrefies, or he purloins his neighbour's share.

As Locke admits, the institution of money alters this equitable-sounding arrangement. Because 'a little piece of yellow metal' is easily transferable and not subject to decay, it enormously extends the remit of value and ownership. He seems optimistic that good government can guard against abuses by the unscrupulous, and promote the increase of wealth and populations. But in fact, even without the institution of money, and still more with it, to make cultivation the criterion of land ownership is hazardous. Locke's theory could be, and was, invoked to justify enclosing common land in England and appropriating the Indians' territories in America. Yet it would also influence Marx's theory of alienation (which holds that, under capitalism, the labourer is estranged from his own humanity because his labour is so piecemeal, mechanical and meaningless), and would be mocked by the 20th century libertarian Robert Nozick, who mused that surely, by Locke's reckoning, if I spill my can of tomato juice in the sea, and its molecules mingle evenly with the water's, I thereby own the ocean.

Locke is enlisted on the side of progressive liberalism – he promoted what Isaiah Berlin called 'negative liberty': the individual's right to freedom from external infringement within her private sphere – her right to free speech, liberty of movement, freedom of worship. But he is also claimed by ruthless libertarian freemarketeers. His labour-mixing notion sounds far less homely and bucolic, far more like proto-capitalism, when he mentions that not just what I, but also 'my servant', cultivate is rightly mine. In Locke's envisaged state, the servant-owning classes stand to own exponentially more than the others.

Recently, there has been much discussion of Locke's financial and political involvement in slavery. He invested in the slave-trading Royal Africa Company, and, although, thanks to his post on the Board of Trade, he had influence over slave-owning Americans, the Carolina constitution that he helped draft contained a clause enjoining that 'Every freedman of the Carolinas has absolute power and authority over his negro slaves'. Chapter 4 in the *Second Treatise* – Of Slavery – is ambiguous, and may only apply to Europeans, ignoring Africans, or even indirectly justify African enslavement as a right in war.

Locke, 'the father of liberalism', was not ideally liberal himself. It would, though, be anachronistic to expect him to have been, and his political philosophy has been liberating.

Key points

- *Essay Concerning Human Understanding* examines what and how we can know.

- Our knowledge consists of ideas, which are the only things we are acquainted with.

- There are no innate ideas; our ideas are solely derived from experience. **Sensation plus reflection** gives rise to knowledge. **Knowledge** is perceiving the agreement and disagreement of any of our ideas.

- We have simple ideas of primary and secondary qualities.

- Primary qualities are the shape, size, weight, and number, of an object, and whether it is in motion or at rest. They exist independent of our perception, and the ideas we have of them resemble the qualities themselves.

- Secondary qualities are what cause various ideas in us, but without resembling those ideas (sound, colour, temperature, for instance). Tertiary qualities are powers an object has to modify the primary and secondary qualities of another object.

- Complex ideas are made by the mind out of simple ones; abstract ideas are i) generalized qualities, ii) generalized (from recurring groups of qualities) 'things'.

- Substance (or a substance) is an indispensable stopgap notion which may refer to an underlying 'something' that we can never perceive – or which may be purely invented.

- Nominal essence is the result of how we classify qualities and things. Real essence may (albeit unperceivably) underlie some of the sets of qualities that we perceive.

- Our knowledge is limited. We can never know the inner nature of things.

- We name our ideas of things, not the things themselves, and, by making abstract ideas and naming them, we create general terms.

- Personal Identity depends on memory. Not only would a hog possessed by the soul of Heliogabalus not be the *same man* – he/it would not be the *same person* either – unless able to *remember having been Heliogabalus*. Locke has begun the dismantling of the Cartesian soul.

- According to Locke's social contract theory, people have natural rights, including to property, even in the state of nature, but a government with just laws makes these rights more secure. An unjust government may be justly unseated. Property is acquired by cultivating land (since we own our own bodies and the labour they perform).

Chapter 4

Benedict de Spinoza (1632–77)

Like the famous duck-rabbit illusion, Spinoza can be seen as one thing, or, alternately, as something quite different – 'an impious atheist' or 'a man drunk with God', a strict determinist or an advocate of self-liberation by means of self-mastery. Mind and body, in his dual-aspect view are the same, yet different. He can be called Baruch, his original Jewish name, or Benedict, the Latin name that he adopted when he was cursed and cast out of the Jewish community (both names mean 'Blessed'). He was a rationalist (someone who

Spinoza can seem full of contradictions – he is both a determinist and an advocate of self-liberation, and he seems obsessed with God yet at other times appears to be an atheist.

makes reason, more than experience, the final arbiter of truth), but he influenced the Romantics, as they (mis)interpreted him, and the 19th-century anti-rationalist Schopenhauer. In his most famous book, the *Ethics* (1677), he conveyed an acute, life-enhancing analysis of the emotions via a rigorous geometrical structure.

Spinoza was unequivocal in defending freedom of conscience, speech and the press, and was the first major thinker to do so – but only one of his books (a critique of Descartes' *Principles of Philosophy*) was published under his name in his lifetime. The anonymous *Theological-Political Treatise* (1670) was soon banned, and condemned by the Dutch Reformed Church as 'the vilest and most sacrilegious book the world has ever seen'. It queried the historical accuracy of biblical narratives, the authenticity of prophecy and miracles, and whether the purported revelations of divine law added anything to those of reason's 'natural light'. Surely, said Spinoza, belief in miracles, although it is invoked to bolster religious belief, should logically lead to atheism since it casts doubt on the God-ordained order of Nature. He objected that theologians 'extort' from scripture 'their own arbitrarily invented ideas, for which they claim divine authority'; religion is just a pretext for compelling others to think

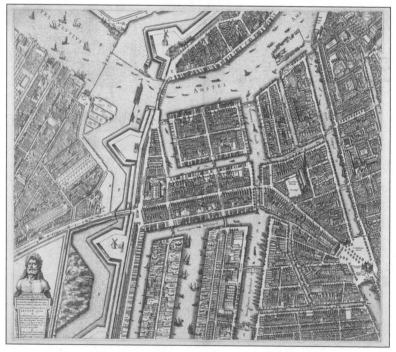

A 17th-century map showing the area of Amsterdam where Spinoza lived after his family fled from the Inquisition.

as they do. And he urged that freedom of expression is not harmful, but essential to public peace, the sovereign's authority and piety.

Recently, in a series of books, Jonathan Israel has proclaimed Spinoza to be the leading figure of Radical Enlightenment; although other historians have riposted that Spinoza's works were hardly read till the end of the 18th century and that the much-bruited 'Spinozism' can hardly count as influential, being more a bigot's term of abuse than an explicit, clearly understood set of opinions.

LIFE

Baruch Spinoza was born on 24 November 1632 into a Portuguese-Jewish family that had fled the Inquisition to live in tolerant Amsterdam. When his father (a merchant in dried fruit) died in 1654, Spinoza renounced any claim to inheritance, and went to live in the house of Franciscus van den Enden, an ex-Jesuit bookseller, who taught him Latin and probably also science and Cartesian philosophy. Two years later, aged 24, Spinoza was expelled from the Jewish synagogue and community with an exceptionally virulent *herem* (writ of banishment), probably for opinions that were heretical in all religions. He soon left Amsterdam.

Often thought of as a solitary ascetic, Spinoza seems in fact to have loved his friends and his country, and enjoyed wine and tobacco. While writing his anonymously published books, he pursued scientific knowledge, especially of optics, and supported himself by making and polishing lenses for spectacles, telescopes and microscopes. Because of his reputation for technical skill and philosophical erudition, he met several of the leading astronomers and mathematicians of the time, and was visited by Leibniz the year before his death. He was offered a professorship at Heidelberg University but refused it, at least partly because he was wary of limits on his freedom to philosophize.

One of his followers, Adrian Koerbagh, was arrested, tortured and died in a grim prison. His teacher, van den Enden, discovered in a conspiracy to assassinate Louis XIV, was hung outside the Bastille. Spinoza's friends and fellow-republicans the de Witt brothers were killed by an Orangist mob, their naked bodies strung up and their livers eaten. On hearing of their murder, Spinoza burst into tears and made a placard saying 'ultimi barbarororum' (worst of barbarians), but his landlord locked him in his lodgings to prevent him going out and displaying it. A few years later, Spinoza was sent on a peace mission to France, and at his return, an angry mob gathered outside his house, calling him a spy and threatening to break in and murder him. He went out and spoke to them of his love for the Dutch Republic, and they dispersed.

Meanwhile, in the *Ethics,* he advocated joy, and that we should detach ourselves from what seems to cause our emotions, and from loving or hating that supposed cause. He died aged 45 of consumption, exacerbated by inhaling glass dust while grinding lenses.

SUBSTANCE, MODE AND ATTRIBUTE IN THE *ETHICS*

'Let us imagine . . . a worm living in the blood . . . being able to distinguish by sight the blood corpuscles, the lymph and so on . . . That worm would be living in the blood as we live in one part of the universe, and it would consider each particle of blood as a whole, and not as a part. It would be unable to know how all the parts are regulated by the general nature of the blood and are compelled by that nature to adapt themselves to one another so as to be mutually harmonized in conformity with a definite law.' This, in one of his letters, is Spinoza's metaphor for the unified, interconnected reality that he argues for in his *Ethics*.

Like most progressive intellectuals of his time, Spinoza was an avid reader of Descartes, and took quite literally Descartes' claim that geometry is the best model of demonstrative argument. *Ethics* sets out, in Euclidean fashion (and in Latin), definitions, axioms, and the propositions which

Euclid's methods were applied by Spinoza to the philosophy of reason as a whole.

purport to follow from them. He begins by defining a set of terms that had been used for metaphysical distinctions ever since Aristotle: 'substance', 'mode' and 'attribute'. 'Substance' he defines in the standard way – as that which exists, and is conceived, independently, in its own right, but he then proceeds to develop the substance-independence notion to its logical conclusion. Most previous philosophers, even if acknowledging (as Descartes did) that strictly speaking there can only be one totally independent substance (God), saw reality as comprising numerous 'created substances'. Spinoza, however, 'proves', by a series of incremental arguments, that it is logically impossible for substance, if self-dependent, to be caused, or limited, by another substance. There can, then, be only one substance; and, by Proposition 11, this is no longer merely 'substance' but rather 'God, or substance consisting of infinite attributes', which necessarily exists; its non-existence (Spinoza argues) being inconceivable.

Apart from lingering Aristotelians, most philosophers of the 17th century took substance itself to be imperceptible. What we perceive and know are its 'modes' or 'accidents' – the properties or changes it manifests and undergoes. You can't see or know a man himself, for instance, *qua* substance; you can only see or know the modes he has and lives through; or rather you see and know the man by way of his modes – that he is brown, black or white, naked or clothed, clever or stupid to varying degrees, healthy or unhealthy, sitting or standing. For Spinoza, however, 'modes', as well as meaning 'properties', turns out to cover entities, facts, events and relations, which are all that can be seen or known of God.

A substance also has 'attributes' – or rather 'an attribute', since this term usually refers to a property that is more intrinsic and essential to a substance than its varying modes. But what Spinoza means by 'attribute' is disputed, different interpretations having different implications for his whole philosophy; and it partly depends on whether he uses the Latin word *tanquam* to mean 'as if' or 'as'.

'Attribute', he says, is 'what the intellect perceives of substance, as if [or 'as'] constituting its essence'. For 'subjectivist' Spinoza scholars, who take tanquam to be 'as if', Spinoza is saying that an attribute is what the intellect *takes as*, but which in fact merely *seems to be*, the essence of a substance (somewhat like Locke's notion of nominal as opposed to real essence). For 'objectivists' (currently in the ascendant) who take tanquam to be 'as', Spinoza is saying that an attribute really *is* the essence of substance. After all, he says that 'clear and distinct' (or 'adequate') ideas truly correspond to things, which surely entails that someone having such ideas can perceive an attribute *as it is.*

The problem for objectivists, however, is how a (or rather, the) substance can have multiple, or at least two, essences.

God or Nature

Spinoza speaks of '*deus sive natura*' ('God or Nature'), as if God and Nature are one and interchangeable. But that might seem to cancel out, and come to much the same as if God did not exist. Many in Spinoza's time, and since, have considered him an atheist. Equally, though, the German Romantic poet Novalis called him 'a God-intoxicated man'. He can be seen as a pantheist (someone who believes that God is immanent in, rather than transcendent to, the whole of reality) or a panentheist (someone who believes that God contains the world as well as being transcendent to it – a position intermediate between deism and pantheism).

There is dispute over every aspect of Spinoza, including in what sense, or even whether, God is everything. In one of his letters, he writes that people who think that the *Theological-Political Treatise* 'rests on the identification of God with Nature (by the latter of which they understand a kind of mass or corporeal matter) are quite mistaken'. Certainly he scorns the standard anthropomorphic idea of God. 'God's will', which is so often invoked to 'explain' unfortunate events, is 'the refuge for ignorance'. God does not will, answer prayers or intervene in natural laws (which are part of what He/It is). To ascribe human properties, such as love or anger, to Him is (says Spinoza) as silly as expecting the Dog Star to resemble 'the animal that barks'.

Even if God or Nature is one – the only – substance, this oneness allows room for manoeuvre. Spinoza borrows a distinction of the Scholastic philosophers – that between *Natura naturans* and *Natura naturata*. This distinction seems to accommodate the Judeo-Christian differentiation between God and His creation, and to imply God's less than total identity with Nature, at least as experienced by us.

Spinoza's monism also accommodates multiplicity: 'From the necessity of the divine nature there must follow infinitely many things in infinitely many ways (that is, everything which can fall under an infinite intellect).' God or substance has an infinite number of finite modes, and these are each (like substance) self-dependent, while yet, as in the worm metaphor, all being part of a single whole. Some scholars claim that Spinoza's monism is materialist, like Hobbes', others that it is a form of idealism (the view that reality is essentially, and only, mental).

GOD AND NATURE

Nature naturing, or Nature as creator, is 'that which is in itself and is conceived through itself, or those attributes of substance which express eternal and infinite essence, that is to say God in so far as He is considered as a free cause'. *Nature natured*, or Nature as effect, is 'everything which follows from the necessity of the nature of God, or of any one of God's attributes, that is to say, all the modes of God's attributes.'

The same, and not the same

Of God's infinite attributes, the only two we know are thought and extension, a duality which sounds Cartesian. But there is more of a gulf between these attributes for Descartes, who saw extension as matter, and thus as something inert which requires to be moved by some other force. For Spinoza, since extension (in one of its infinite modes, at least) is 'motion-and-rest', it is therefore already animated. And the ideas which 'the mind forms because it is a thinking thing' are 'concepts', rather than passive imprints, as in Descartes, Locke and Hume: Spinoza wants to emphasize that the mind is active.

Whether the attributes of thought and extension *are* (on an objectivist interpretation), or only *seem to be* (on a subjectivist one), the essence of God/Nature, these attributes are not in fact different – merely conceived under different aspects. The causal sequence of mental and physical events is 'coincident in Nature' not because they are correlated but because 'substance thinking and substance extended are one and the same substance'. Any finite mode (me, the dog, a palm tree) is both mental and physical (as a unit, not as a Cartesian conjunction of attributes), yet can only be apprehended as one or the other – rather in the way that you can look at the same drawing, and see it as portraying a duck or a rabbit alternately, not simultaneously.

Spinoza and Mind/Body Identity Theories

It is hard to know how exactly this mental/physical unit can be 'comprehended now through one attribute, now through the other'. What do the identity, and the dual comprehension of it, come to? How does it work? In a letter seeking to explain this, Spinoza gives two examples of 'how one and the same thing can be signified by two names'. The same thing can be referred to as 'plane surface' and as 'white surface', he writes. The former term classifies something in a purely geometrical way, while the latter considers the same thing, but in the context of how it appears to someone looking at it. Similarly, you can refer to the Third Patriarch as either 'Israel' or 'Jacob', depending on the context. Spinoza here seems to appeal to what, in the 20th century, Gottlob Frege would formulate as the difference between 'reference' (the thing that a word refers to) and 'sense' (what the word means). And some philosophers, in the ongoing 21st-century debate about if, and how, what we call mental states are somehow physical, claim that Spinoza's 'dual aspect theory' provides the structure for solving this problem. Identity Theorists of the 1950s argued that although when saying someone is angry you do not *mean* that they are having a particular brain state, it is in fact a yet-to-be-pinpointed type of brain state that you are *referring to*, for that is what anger will turn out to *be*.

A problem for Spinoza and for Identity Theories, however, is that Israel and Jacob can each be identified as 'Third Patriarch' (the role they have in common), since 'they' are the same *person*, whereas the terms 'feeling of anger' and 'brain state of a certain type' do not provide two perspectives on the same entity, because there is no entity or event that both terms pick out; no category that subsumes 'feeling of anger' as well as 'brain state', or applies to both or either terms. Each is apparently of such a disparate, incommensurable species as to prohibit 'causal intercourse' with one another (as Donald Davidson put it in the 1970s). To explain the cause of someone's brain state involves discerning and tracing successive configurations of bits of neural matter; while to explain the cause of an

The Third Patriarch (right) can be referred to as either 'Israel' or 'Jacob' depending on the context.

In both the diagrams, the dotted lines are what we think of as *either* mental *or* physical causal links. The full lines are the real causal links.

SPINOZA'S MONISM

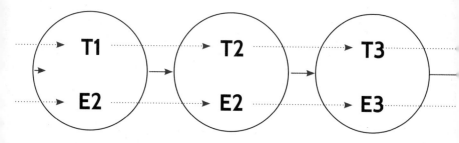

It is unclear exactly what they amount to, for Spinoza, but he, unlike Davidson, insists on their indissoluble oneness during life.

DAVIDSON'S ANOMALOUS MONISM

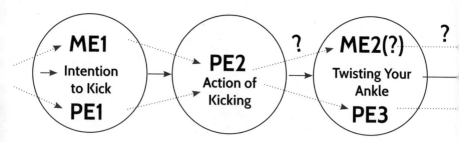

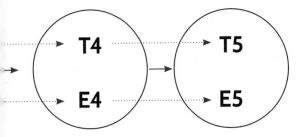

T= Thought (idea)

E = Extension (motion-and-rest)

Circles represent mental/physical units

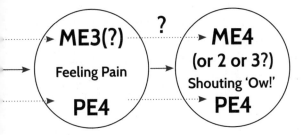

ME = Mental Event

PE = Physical Event

Circles represent mental/physical events – or purely physical ones.

angry feeling involves discerning and tracing whole realms of meaning, association and history spanning the life and culture of the angry person.

If Spinoza is of doubtful help to Type Identity Theorists, perhaps, according to Davidson, he anticipates Token Identity Theory because he is 'ontologically monistic [holding that everything that exists is of the same stuff] but conceptually dualistic'. '*As described*' (in mental or physical terms), a feeling of anger and a brain state each respectively 'retains allegiance to its proper source of evidence', says Davidson, so they cannot be jointly subsumed under a strict psycho-physical law or a *type* identity. Yet precisely that impossibility – given that, in practice, they do causally interact (my anger results in my hitting the thief) – entails that, *ad hoc* and at a particular time, they must in fact be the very same unclassifiable thing. Davidson claims that his Token Identity Theory is 'Spinozistic'.

Yet Davidson's Anomalous Monism persuasively argues that it is the very undeniability of causal – if lawlessly causal – interaction between a prior mental event and a subsequent physical one (and vice versa) that demonstrates mental/physical identity; whereas Spinoza starts at the other end. Just before his extensive discussion of how 'mind and body are one and the same thing' comes a Proposition (Book 3, Prop 2) declaring that the body can't cause the mind to think, nor the mind cause the body to move or rest. Davidson's conclusion is in fact Spinoza's presupposition – and might, at first glance, even seem to contradict it. But Spinoza is of course only denying mental-physical causation because, or to the extent that, mind and body *are one*. He has already said (mysteriously) that the mind is the idea of the body, and his aim, like Davidson's, is to refute, while doing justice to them, Cartesian dualism and the problems of mental/physical interactionism. He criticizes Descartes, along with the Stoics, for considering the will as a faculty with 'absolute authority', and ridicules his pseudo-scientific notion that the pineal gland actuates the 'animal spirits' while itself being actuated by the soul.

Spinoza would agree with Davidson that the mental/physical unit that integrally thinks, moves and rests can causally interact with other mental/physical units, including itself in the future. Ultimately indeed Spinoza's monism is more consistent than Davidson's, in which some events would appear to be purely physical.

WINDOWLESS MONADS

Gottfried Leibniz (below) had a clever way of getting round mental/physical causal interaction. If you could see the 'shapes and motions' in someone's brain, he said, you would be none the wiser about what is being perceived, and how. There must, then, be ultimate self-subsisting substances that do perceive, are self-activating and do not occupy space. Every physical thing is really an assemblage of these extensionless points ('monads'), and is unified and powered by its dominant monad.

This 'could be called the soul'. 'Like a world apart, independent of every other thing except God', it is 'windowless' – has no causal influence on, or from, anything outside itself. Due to an

advance causation, arranged by God, it has its own intrinsic predetermined nature, and everything that ever happens to it can only be the consequences of that. Yet because it 'expresses' and mirrors the world – if confusedly, from its own perspective – its self-contained life-history unfolds in 'pre-established harmony' with that of every other monad.

It sounds odd, Spinoza concedes, to talk as if people build a temple, for instance, without being 'determined [caused] by the mind'; but we don't yet know, he says, all that the body can do when not mentally determined. This might sound inadvertently dualist, but in the same Scholium in the *Ethics* Part 3, Spinoza urges that experience shows how indivisibly unified mind and body are. If the body is sluggish, the mind can't think properly; the feverish person and the chatterbox cannot control their garrulousness; to act on 'a mental decision' requires memory, which is quite outside conscious control. 'Those who believe that they speak, or keep silent or do anything from free mental decision are dreaming with their eyes open.' Although we believe ourselves to be free, we only know what we do, not the causes for our doing it. Experience, however, should tell us that 'mental decisions are nothing more than the appetites themselves,' which vary according to the body's variations. Mental volition does not cause physical action, but is part of it. Desire to move is interwoven in movement.

DETERMINISM

Spinoza is usually considered a determinist (believing that everything, including the human mind, is subject to cause and effect).

At the beginning of Part 3 (The Origin and Nature of the Affects), he announces that he will pursue the same geometrical method when dealing with human actions and appetites as with any other finite modes, and will consider human affects, such as hatred, anger and envy, 'just as if I were considering lines, planes, or bodies'. He will not, as other philosophers do, 'consider man in Nature as a kingdom within a kingdom' – a sovereign state that has its own dominion of free will – and as something that 'disturbs, rather than follows, the order of Nature', but simply as an interdependent part of the whole. For 'there should be one and the same method of understanding the nature of all things whatsoever, namely, through Nature's universal laws and rules'.

It sounds as if, whether considered as a conglomeration of ideas, or as a form of motion-and-rest, the human is not an agent but a thoroughfare for cause and effect, just as much as any other finite mode, whether stone, star, reed or fish, and in much the same way.

Famously, Spinoza puts a stone on the same level as a human. 'A stone receives from the impulsion of an external cause a fixed quantity of

Spinoza places a stone and a human being on the same level - like the stone, we are unaware of what causes our desires, and our actions are determined.

motion whereby it will necessarily continue to move when the impulsion of the external cause has ceased'; if the stone, as it moved, could think (Spinoza says), it would 'know' that it is 'endeavouring, in so far as in it lies, to continue in motion', and will think that it is 'completely free, and that it continues in motion for no other reason than that it so wishes'. All that our sense of having free will amounts to is an illusion, like the stone's, that we are acting freely, because we are unaware of what causes our desires. But 'there is no absolute or free will. The mind is determined to this or that volition by a cause which is also determined by another cause, and this again by another, and so on *ad infinitum.*'

Yet in a sense the stone is not deluded at all. Each finite mode, human or non-human, possesses a *conatus*: a striving 'to persevere in its own being'. 'Mental decision on the one hand, and the appetite and physical state of the body on the other hand, are simultaneous in nature, or rather they are one and the same thing which, when considered under the attribute of thought and explained in terms of it, we call decision, and when considered under the attribute of extension and deduced from the laws of motion-and-rest, we call a physical cause.'

Spinoza's *conatus* is sometimes compared to Schopenhauer's Will, the blind striving force that blows through, and is, the whole of reality, or to Freud's avid libido; but it is much more differentiated and specific to its possessor than the supposed equivalents in these later thinkers. The *conatus* of each finite mode is what makes it what it is, for its *conatus* 'is nothing but the essence of the thing itself', its own idiosyncratic drive for self-preservation.

Non-human appetites and drives are desires when consciously recognized, but being aware of them makes little difference. Rather than desiring, seeking and striving for what we judge in advance to be good, we tend to judge to be good whatever we feel compelled to strive for, seek and desire.

Good and evil

It seems odd for a determinist to write about ethics, when the very notion of ethics invariably presupposes freedom of will; but as usual Spinoza stretches his own parameters, so much so as often to appear inconsistent.

At the beginning of Part 4 (Of Human Bondage), he says that man, because he has convinced himself that everything that exists is made for him, is therefore compelled to explain nature in terms of good and evil, even though these terms convey nothing definite about the properties of things so described. 'For one and the same thing may at the same time be both good and evil or indifferent'; music, for instance, being good to someone melancholy, bad to the mourner, indifferent to the deaf. This seems to chime in with Spinoza's notion of all-embracing oneness; for, if God or Nature is everything, how can anything be distinguished as either good or bad? It also sounds like the Stoic idea that (in Hamlet's words) 'nothing is either good or bad but thinking makes it so' – that things and events are variably and comparatively, rather than intrinsically and objectively beneficial or harmful; benefit and harm, therefore, consisting merely in our own subjective response to them, which we can control.

SPINOZA THE PANPSYCHIST

Because of his view that everything has mental as well physical attributes (since both are ultimately the same, but seen from different aspects), Spinoza is often considered to be a panpsychist (someone of the view that everything in nature is, in some way, and to some degree, conscious).

Yet almost immediately after having claimed 'good' and 'evil' to be merely local and comparative, Spinoza declares the terms 'good' and 'bad' to be indispensable to us in practice. He goes on to define 'good' as 'that which we certainly know is useful to us' and to be 'everything that we certainly know to be the means for our approaching nearer to the model of human nature we set before us'. The latter definition may perhaps gesture at some sort of ethical objectivity and standardization, but it is unclear how the 'model' is to be formed and agreed on. Spinoza's ethics are sometimes branded Subjectivist (treating moral principles as just a matter of personal taste) and egoistic.

Spinoza anticipates the idea of the 'invisible hand of the market' when he suggests that acting on self-interest creates advantages for humanity as a whole.

Perhaps, however, Spinoza means that good (usefulness), although not invariable and homogeneous, is not arbitrary either; that there is in fact objective truth, and potential 'certain knowledge', as to what the good – for each person, in each situation, as part of the whole – precisely is. He says, too, that when men live conformably to reason, they 'necessarily do those things that are good to human nature, and consequently for every single man'. Thus 'it is when each is most devoted to seeking his own advantage that men are of most advantage to one another'. He almost seems to anticipate Adam Smith's idea of the invisible hand that strokes self-interest into general profit.

Another apparent inconsistency is that although he uses the Stoic idea that our application of 'good' or 'bad' is non-uniform and subjective, therefore in a sense unreal, he criticizes the Stoics for claiming that emotions depend entirely on our will. Of course he denies that there is a faculty of will, and that it is free, but his definition of an emotion as 'an inadequate or confused idea' – a sort of correctable misapprehension – seems Stoic-like. And doesn't *correcting* require will?

What perhaps distinguishes Spinoza from the Stoics who emphasize will-power is his own emphasis on self-knowledge. Anyone who has

Like Freud, Spinoza believed that we could purge our unconscious desires by being made aware of them.

an 'adequate idea' (an idea that is complete and true) of what drives them, and therefore of what their emotions are, can (according to Spinoza) thereby dissolve those emotions and partially shrug off their bondage. A compulsive emotion (a 'passion' or state that we involuntarily undergo) 'ceases to be a passion as soon as we form a clear and distinct idea of it'. He is thought to have anticipated Freud's panacea that, by bringing unconscious motives and desires into awareness, we can purge them.

But, unlike Freud, he believes that we can in principle live 'according to the guidance of reason', and that someone who does so acts 'absolutely from the laws of his own nature'. Greater knowledge of yourself and your *conatus* brings greater power to act; and Spinoza equates power with virtue, and virtue with living to the top of your bent. Powerlessness (he says) consists in being swayed by external things, rather than by reason and by what your own intrinsic nature 'demands'.

It is, however, only 'the wise man' who can attain 'adequate ideas'; and the self-mastery that results from having them will be limited. Unlike the Stoics, more like Freud, Spinoza says that 'a man is necessarily always subject to passive emotions, and . . . follows the common order of Nature, and obeys it, and accommodates himself to it as far as the nature of things requires'.

Far more acutely than the Stoics or Freud, Spinoza describes and explains the mental/physical entanglement that constitutes emotion, and how it creates a useful (or harmful) feedback mechanism. Although emotion as a 'passive experience' is a confused idea, it is a potent one – an idea 'whereby the mind affirms of its body, or any part of it, a greater or less power of existence than before, as a result of which the mind is swayed towards having one particular thought rather than another'. The idea/emotion, in fact, is a self-fulfilling prophecy that changes not only the emoter's physical state but their thoughts and their whole world, enhancing or diminishing their vigour and sense of life.

Joy, for Spinoza, is a state of the entire body by which its power of action is intensified, and which is therefore good. Sorrow, which diminishes or restrains this power, is evil. Like Hume, he thinks that 'nothing but a gloomy and sad superstition forbids enjoyment'. The highest good is the 'intellectual love of God', which is achieved by someone who 'clearly and distinctly understands himself and his emotions'. Despite mocking the childish anthropomorphism of ascribing will or emotion to God, this (scarcely achievable) 'intellectual love of God' turns out to be the very love with which God loves himself.

'It is in the nature of reason to perceive things under the aspect of eternity,' says Spinoza. Unlike Descartes' *Meditations*, which could be said to start with the worm's-eye view of the solitary thinker, Spinoza's *Ethics* begins with substance, which turns out to be God. By the end, it seems that, despite being subject to causation and time, the human mind is potentially capable of knowing itself, the body and God 'sub specie aeternitatis'; even (Spinoza suggests) of attaining immortality.

But memory and imagination cease when the body does, he says, so even if 'something of the human mind remains which is eternal', its immortality must be fairly nugatory. No redemption, no personal relationship to the divine. Under one of his multiple aspects, Spinoza can be seen as herald of the death of God.

Key points

- Spinoza's Ethics is set out in geometric proofs, and begins with definitions of substance, mode and attribute.

- If a substance is what is 'in itself', then it cannot be caused, or limited, by another substance. The one self-caused, infinite substance (God or Nature) is both *Natura naturans* (Nature as cause) and *Natura naturata* (Nature as effect).

- The modifications (modes) of God or Nature are everything that we normally call things, facts, events, relations.

- Two of God's attributes – thought and extension – are conceived of in different ways, but are really the same, and are part of the same causal chain.

- The essence of every creature and every thing [sic] is a *conatus*, a striving to persevere in its own being. A *conatus* is both mental and physical – both will and bodily cause.

- Spinoza's dual aspect theory is (disputably) said to anticipate Davidson's form of Token Identity Theory.

- For humans, good and evil don't truly exist since everything is part of God. 'Good' refers to what is advantageous, and what promotes the approved model of human nature.

- Although probably a determinist, Spinoza argues that we can be in some way freed from our emotions if we attain knowledge of what causes them and what they are.

- To achieve knowledge of ourselves as we are under the aspect of eternity is to possess the 'intellectual love of God'.

Chapter 5

George Berkeley (1685–1753)

B erkeley is famous for his *idealism* (in its philosophical meaning: a belief that reality is fundamentally mental rather than physical) and *immaterialism* (the belief, which idealism may entail, that material things don't exist). A Church of Ireland bishop, he also wrote on religion and theology, the psychology of vision, maths, economics, physics and medicine. He is sometimes excluded from accounts of the Enlightenment because he can be seen as going backwards, trying to staunch the tide unleashed by Descartes and Locke that he sensed to be flowing towards scepticism and atheism.

George Berkeley was a Church of Ireland bishop renowned for his idealism.

As with any great philosopher, he is important not because we think he's right (practically no one does) but for what he makes us puzzled about. He drew attention to how the world is in some sense mind-dependent, to how, as William James would say at the beginning of the 20th century, 'the trail of the human serpent is . . . over everything'.

LIFE

George Berkeley was born in 1685 into an Anglo-Irish family in Kilkenny. He studied at Trinity College, Dublin, where he became a tutor and Greek lecturer and wrote a mathematical treatise; in 1709, he was ordained a Church of Ireland deacon. His greatest philosophical work was done before the age of 28. *An Essay towards a New Theory of Vision* (1709), discussing the perception of distance, and problems in sight and touch, proved controversial; *A Treatise Concerning the Principles of Human Knowledge* (1710) earned him respect, ridicule and a doctor's diagnosis of insanity. Visiting London in 1713 for the publication of *Three Dialogues between Hylas and Philonous*, Berkeley made illustrious literary friends, including the poet Alexander Pope, essayists Joseph Addison and Richard Steele and the satirist Jonathan Swift, who was said to have kept Berkeley waiting on his doorstep, insisting that surely, according to his own philosophy, he could as easily walk through a closed door as an open one.

Between 1716 and 1721, Berkeley travelled in Europe as chaplain or tutor, writing copious travel notes, including a description of Mount Vesuvius erupting. He was Dean of Dromore from 1721 to 1724, then Dean of Derry. But hating the Old World's decadence, and hopeful

Berkeley recorded his travels in Europe in writing, including a description of the eruption of Mount Vesuvius.

about the uncorrupted New World, he was determined to found a college in Bermuda at which 'the savage Americans' could be converted to Christianity and English settlers, educated with them, could be reformed. Having been granted a charter for his college by George I, he went to America with his new wife Ann in 1728, and bought a farm on Rhode Island where they lived for three years. But the promised funding never materialised.

Returning to London, Berkeley helped care for abandoned children. From 1734 to 1752, while being Bishop of Cloyne, he tried to forge links with Irish Catholics, and wrote polemics about the plight of the Irish poor, as well as tackling it in practice. He obsessively administered tarwater to the local people – a disgusting pine tar infusion that he considered a remedy for all ills, and philosophised about in *Siris* (1744). On retiring from the bishopric, he, his wife and daughter moved to Oxford where his son was studying. He died a year later.

PHILOSOPHICAL AIMS

Seventeenth-century science, via Descartes and Locke, engendered the philosophical theory of Indirect Realism: that what we immediately perceive are 'ideas' (sense impressions), many of which (ideas of secondary qualities) do not resemble the world as it is. Berkeley was afraid that such theories would lead to scepticism. He also foresaw that, despite Descartes' personal faith and assurance to the clerics, the 'mechanical philosophy' would result in God being relegated to mere kick-starter of the universe (deism), and ultimately to being redundant (atheism). Berkeley sought to scotch scepticism by obliterating the distinction between appearance and reality (which is what gives rise to scepticism in the first place). In a magnificent double whammy, he postulates an immaterial world, and makes the existence and perception of it depend on God. He is adamant that he is appealing to common sense, although he was considered mad in his time; and urges that whereas other philosophers are being elitist, he is catering to ordinary people. He aims to produce a theory that is 'agreeable to common sense and remote from scepticism', though admits that it is necessary 'to think with the learned, and speak with the vulgar'.

Berkeley does not argue systematically, and scholars endlessly dispute precisely what he is saying or claiming, and whether some of it (however interpreted) could be as preposterous as it sounds. Below is an attempt at charting his arguments.

Starting point

1) Like Descartes and Locke, Berkeley believes that the things immediately perceived are ideas which exist only in the mind and that all our knowledge is derived from our ideas. Like Locke (but unlike Descartes), he does not believe in innate ideas, and is always categorized as an empiricist.

2) Again like Locke, Berkeley believes that because we observe certain sorts of ideas regularly accompanying one another, we give the cluster a name, and it is thus 'reputed as one thing'. Thus 'collections of ideas constitute a stone, a tree, a book, and the like sensible things'.

But Berkeley blames Locke's theory of abstract ideas for making us separate in thought things that are in fact inseparable – primary from secondary qualities, and sensible things from their being perceived. Locke's theory is false, he says. Each word has to correspond to a particular idea, so how is it possible to extrapolate from the particularities of all men, for instance, an abstract idea of man? Would we be thinking of a man who is white, black or tawny; tall, small or medium-sized? (We do, however, have general ideas, he says, thanks to the way we use words).

DISMANTLING THE PHYSICAL WORLD

1) Berkeley's objections to primary and secondary qualities

Berkeley disagrees with Descartes and Locke about the distinction between primary and secondary qualities (see p.60). Instead, he argues that the so-called primary qualities would be just as dependent on, and relative to, us as secondary ones, therefore equally 'in the mind'.

a) The so-called primary and secondary qualities are 'inseparably united', and cannot be abstracted from one another. How could something have length but no colour, or solidity without feeling a certain way to the touch, and so on?

b) Size, bulk and shape, movement or stillness, which are all supposed to be independent of the observer, are in fact observer-relative, and bound up with position and point of view, and standard of measurement. Something that a human would find tiny, says Berkeley, a mite would find huge. Locke could rightly reply that the mite and the human could nonetheless agree on a common unit of measurement – a miteimetre, perhaps. The primary quality of size would thus continue to be mathematically objective.

c) Number is relative, since how we differentiate things depends on the category we put them into (something can be seen as one book, as several pages, and/or as numerous lines of print, for instance).

2) Berkeley demolishes physical substance

Descartes claimed (and Locke may have done, ambiguously) that substance underlies the primary and secondary qualities (matter in general, and/or a particular 'support' of particular qualities). Berkeley demands:

a) How could matter cause us to have ideas, since it is inactive? (Descartes' dualism made problematic how physical can interact with mental stuff, and he never satisfactorily explained this. Berkeley was impressed by the Cartesian cleric Malebranche, whose answer was that matter is inactive but that each time we want to move our bodies it is God that actually causes the movement. Like Malebranche, Berkeley believed that causation involved the activity of willing.)

b) How can we know what we can't know? How are Descartes, Locke and the rest entitled to assume there is anything material outside our ideas? Since we have knowledge 'only of our sensations', we would have the same perceptions whether or not there is anything outside our ideas. Berkeley uses the argument from illusion (see p.58) – not (as Indirect Realists do) to prove that we have ideas (sense data), but to prove that there cannot be physical things or qualities which cause our ideas. In *A Treatise concerning the Principles of Human Knowledge* he wrote, 'Though it were possible that solid, figured, moveable substances may exist without [outside] the mind, corresponding to the ideas we have of bodies, yet how is it possible for us to know this? Either we must know it by sense, or by reason. As for our senses, by them we have the knowledge only of our sensations, ideas, or those things that are perceived by sense,

Berkeley took inspiration from the cleric-philosopher Nicholas Malebranche.

call them what you will: but they do not inform us that things exist without the mind, or unperceived, like to those which are perceived. This the materialists themselves acknowledge. It remains therefore that if we have any knowledge at all of external things, it must be by reason, inferring their existence from what is immediately perceived by sense. But I do not see what reason can induce us to believe the existence of bodies without the mind, from what we perceive, since the very patrons of matter themselves do not pretend, that there is any necesssary connexion betwixt them and our ideas. I say, it is granted on all hands (and what happens in dreams, frenzies, and the like, puts it beyond dispute) that it is possible we might be affected with all the ideas we have now, though no bodies existed without, resembling them. Hence it is evident the supposition of external bodies is not necessary for the producing our ideas.'

3) Berkeley collapses qualities into ideas

a) How can Descartes and Locke reconcile the claim that our ideas resemble qualities outside us with the claim that ideas are the only things we can perceive? 'For how can it be known, that the things which are perceived, are conformable to those which are not perceived, or exist without [outside] the mind?' asks Berkeley. Two things cannot be said to be alike or unalike till they have been compared. There is nothing conceivable that ideas could be likenesses of, he argues, except other mind-dependent entities.

b) How, on the other hand, could we have ideas which are *unlike* what is alleged to cause them (light-waves, vibrations, chemicals)? In the *Dialogues*, Hylas (believer in a material, physical world) offers Locke's account (scientific but also dualist) of sound: that a motion in the air, when striking the eardrum, causes a vibration, which 'by the auditory nerves being communicated to the brain, the soul is thereupon affected with the sensation called sound'. He asks Philonous (lover of mind) to distinguish 'between sound as it is perceived by us, and as it is in itself . . . Is it not evident, those accidents or modes belong only to sensible sound, or *sound* in the common acceptation of the word, but not to *sound* in the real and philosophic sense, which, as I just now told you, is nothing but a certain motion of the air?'

Philonous replies: 'It seems that there are two sorts of sound, the one vulgar, or that which is heard, the other philosophical and real . . . It should follow then, according to you, real sounds may possibly be seen or felt, but never heard . . . But can you think it no more than a philosophical paradox, to say that real sounds are never heard, and that the idea of them is obtained by some other sense . . . It seems [according to Hylas that] there are two sorts of sound, the one vulgar, or that which is heard, the other philosophical and real . . . But how can that which is sensible be like that which is insensible? Can a real thing in itself invisible be like a colour; or a real thing which is not audible, be like a sound? In a word, can anything be like a sensation or idea, but another sensation or idea?'

In saying that it is meaningless to speak of an unheard sound, or an unsmelled smell, Berkeley is not just saying the obvious; few philosophers would disagree with Hylas that vibrations, ear-drums, auditory nerves and so on are necessary for a sound to be heard. But although Berkeley/Philonous *does* disagree, he rightly reminds us: 'There was an odour, that is, it was smelled; there was a sound, that is to say, it was heard; a colour or figure, and it was perceived by sight or touch. This is all that I can understand by these and the like expressions.' When someone says that they are hearing a sound (an explosion, a tune, a creak) or smelling a smell (a rose, putrefaction), what they are talking about is *what the sound or smell is like* (and sometimes what that sound or smell implies concerning the thing from which it may emanate). They are similarly invoking the quiddity or significance of a smell or a sound when reporting that someone else has smelled or heard something. What they are *not* doing is speaking or thinking about the physical components/ events of sound-hearing (they may even be altogether ignorant of the science involved).

Physicalists would agree with Berkeley/Philonous that the biological account of sound *does not mean* 'sound'. But they sometimes seem to agree with Hylas that physical occurrences *are* the sound, the very fact of sound itself, rather than being its cause or correlate. What philosophers such as Thomas Nagel and David Chalmers stress is the 'explanatory gap' to be bridged – the cross-over from physical things and events to someone's hearing a sound – and that the latter and former are not identical. (Berkeley, of course, is, or intends to be, an idealist, rather than a dualist, so he takes the argument in a different direction.)

4) Ideas or groups of ideas exist only as and when we perceive them

In the *Principles* sections 22–3 and the *Dialogues*, Berkeley uses an argument that he is so pleased with that it has been called 'the Master Argument'. Here is part of it:

'I am content to put the whole upon this issue; if you can but conceive it possible for one extended moveable substance, or in general, for any one idea or any thing like an idea, to exist otherwise than in a mind perceiving it, I shall readily give up the cause ... But say you, surely there is nothing easier than to imagine trees, for instance, in a park, or books existing in a closet, and no body by to perceive them. I answer, you may so, there is no difficulty in it: but *what* is all this, I beseech you, more than framing in your mind certain ideas which you call *books* and *trees*, and at the same time omitting to frame the idea of any one that may perceive them? But do not you your self perceive or think of them all the while? This therefore is nothing to the purpose: it only shows you have the power of imagining or forming ideas in your mind; but it doth not shew that you can conceive it possible, the objects of your thought may exist without the mind: to make out this, it is necessary that you conceive them existing unconceived or unthought of, which is a manifest repugnancy. When we do our utmost to conceive the existence of external bodies, we are all the while only contemplating our own ideas. But the mind taking no notice of itself, is deluded to think it can and doth conceive bodies existing unthought of or without the mind; though at the same time they are apprehended by or exist in it self.'

Is he saying that if we try to think of something unthought of, we have to think of it? That would be a very weak, indeed false, contention. Scholars argue over what he means, and its cogency (see Problems and Inconsistencies in Berkeley, p.110).

5) Perceiving, willing minds and their perceptions are all that exist

'As to what is said of the absolute existence of unthinking things without any relation to their being perceived, that seems perfectly unintelligible. Their esse is percipi [their to-be is to be perceived], nor is it possible they should have any existence, out of the minds or thinking things which perceive them.' 'To exist is to be perceived or to perceive or to will, that is to act', Berkeley writes (in Latin) in his Notebooks. He seems to be saying that what we perceive or imagine is indistinguishable from the state/action of perceiving or imagining. That helps him to dismantle the physical world, and to remove scepticism by obliterating the gap between appearance and reality. It is not just that the things we perceive are as we perceive them. The perceivings are the things.

So we are left with a cosmos consisting only of ideas and the minds that perceive these ideas – or we would be had Berkeley not brought in God.

6) God

As presented so far, Berkeley's argument would have to say that if a tree fell in the forest, and there were no hearing creature in the vicinity, the falling would make no sound – except that he seems to have also said that no trees, nor any other physical objects, exist. If our ideas are not produced by 'external bodies', he seems to have left us with only ideas (or sense data, as they would come to be called in the 20th century) – the position of phenomenalism.

However, Berkeley, like Descartes, says that although he can use his will to summon up imaginary ideas or memories, 'whatever power I have over my own thoughts, I find the ideas perceived by sense have not a like dependence on my will'. 'Sensible ideas' are often involuntary, therefore caused. Caused by what? Only a mind has causal power, according to Berkeley (see 2a). He uses the passivity of perception argument (as do Descartes and Locke) – not, however, to argue for the existence of the external world, but for the existence of God: 'Whence I conclude, not that they have no real existence, but that seeing they depend not on my thought, and have an existence distinct from being perceived by me, there must be some other mind wherein they exist. As sure therefore, as the sensible world really exists, so sure is there an infinite omnipresent spirit who contains and supports it.'

7) Minds

Right from the outset of the *Principles*, Berkeley talks of ideas as objects of knowledge, and talks, too, of 'something that knows and perceives them'. 'This perceiving, active being is what I call mind, spirit, soul or myself,' he writes. But he has to admit that the individual cannot 'strictly' be said to have an idea of *their own* mind, let alone of anyone else's, since ideas occur *in* minds. Judging by his *Notebooks*, in fact, he at one point had a view of self similar to Hume's – that the self can only be the collection of ideas that the individual is currently having.

DR SAMUEL JOHNSON ON BERKELEY

Dr Johnson, an 18th-century figure renowned for robust common sense, was exasperated by Berkeley's theory. 'I refute it thus,' he famously said, kicking a large stone. But he didn't *refute* the theory; he merely rejected it. Because we always favour sight over our other senses, we (and Johnson) assume the stone is like Macbeth's dagger: perceptible only by sight, not touchable. But a stone in Berkeley's universe is indistinguishable from one in Locke's. It not only looks grey and green, lichen-covered, unevenly shaped, but *feels solid.*

Yet although denying *physical* substance, Berkeley asserts that there are *mental* substances. He collapses qualities into ideas, but hangs onto the Aristotelian-Scholastic concept that qualities necessarily 'inhere' in a substance (a concept invoked by Descartes, and perhaps also, if ambivalently, by Locke). For Berkeley, however, the substance which the ideas/qualities inhere in is a mind. He says that each person has, if not an idea, then a 'notion' of their own mind and the minds of other people, although he only added the concept of 'notion' to the 1734 editions of the *Principles* and the *Dialogues*.

Presumably, then, each human is a mental substance that is somehow linked to, and enclosed in, a cluster of ideas (their body). They can perceive their own body, and other people can perceive it too, and have a 'notion' of their mind. This, to all intents and purposes, involves the same sort of body-bounded dualism as Descartes, and a Cartesian process of inference from bodies and behaviour to minds, an inference gleaned from the physical. Whatever Descartes or Berkeley say about the mind not occupying space, the only way my mind is discrete from yours or his is that it is indeed 'within', somehow enclosed in a body; and this also ensures the privacy and privileged accessibility of its thoughts. And surely the body-constituting ideas, the body-enclosed minds, and the ideas that the minds are having all, whether immaterial or not, need to exist in a shared public space.

So, Berkeley held that everything in the world is mental – God, human minds, and (collections of) ideas, 'the existence of which consists of being perceived'. Minds are active, ideas passive. God, an infinite mind, directly (without the unnecessary mediation of any material substance) causes our finite human minds to perceive all the 'sensible ideas' we have. He sustains ideas in being when we do not perceive them. Berkeley insists that to say everything we perceive is ideas is not to detract from the existence or reality of things. Nothing is taken nothing away from our experience, since all we experience are ideas in any case.

8) Berkeley's science

There is, as he admits, a problem for him, given his assertions that 'ideas have nothing powerful or operative in them' and that God is the only source of causal power. Surely all the 'order and connexion' which is

BERKELEY'S IDEALISM
MENTAL (there is no physical world)

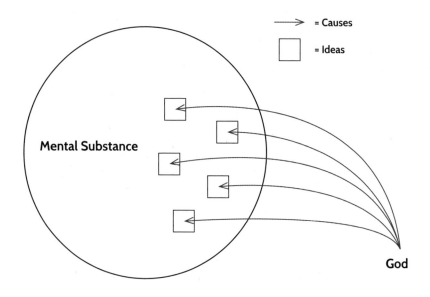

indeed 'like to that of cause and effect', and the 'curious organization of plants, and the admirable mechanism in the parts of animals', are superfluous and misleading. Why does God take 'round-about methods of effecting things by instruments and machines, which no one can deny might have been effected by the mere command of his will'?

Berkeley's answer is that what seem to be causal relations are signifying signs in God's language, which 'admonish us' so that we can avoid whatever may be hurtful and destructive of 'our bodies' and gain 'a sort of foresight, which enables us to regulate our actions for the benefit of life'. We learn by experience that certain ideas are attended with certain other ideas, and these regularities 'are called the Laws of Nature'. Thanks to a connection taught us by experience, we sow seeds in spring and reap the crop in autumn. Similarly, distance and space ('outness') are not there to be perceived; rather, they are 'suggested to our thoughts by certain visible

BERKELEY'S MORE REALIST POSITION
MENTAL (there is no physical world)

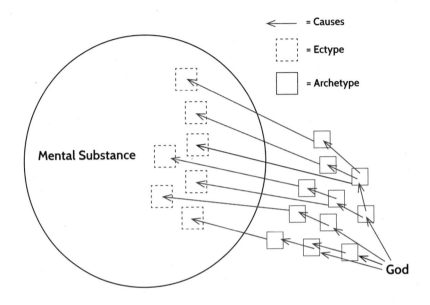

ideas and sensations attending vision' which indicate 'that ideas of touch will be imprinted in our minds at such and such distances of time, and in consequence of such and such actions.' Berkeley does think science, and what passes for scientific explanation, is useful – as long as we bear in mind that scientists are contemplating signs rather than causes.

> 'We are chained to a body, that is to say, our perceptions are connected with corporeal motions. By the Law of our Nature we are affected upon every alteration in the nervous parts of our sensible body: which sensible body rightly considered, is nothing but a complexion of such qualities or ideas, as have no existence distinct from being perceived by a mind.' (*Dialogues* 3, 241)

DR JOHNSON'S ERROR

Of Dr Johnson, Boswell wrote: 'Being in company with a gentleman who thought fit to maintain Dr Berkeley's ingenious philosophy, that nothing exists but as perceived by some mind; when the gentleman was going away, Johnson said to him, "Pray, sir, don't leave us; for we may perhaps forget to think of you, and then you will cease to exist."' In fact Johnson was doubly wrong about Berkeley's position: the man's mind would persist because minds are persisting substances; and the cluster of ideas that constitute his body would, whether or not it was being observed, be maintained in existence by God.

Problems and inconsistencies in Berkeley

1) Berkeley's 'Master Argument' is so cryptic (and disappointing) that it has been endlessly interpreted (and criticized). He is often accused of conflating two meanings of 'idea' – idea as the act or event of perceiving, and idea as what the perception is of – and thus equivocating between idea-as-form and idea-as-content.

Descartes skilfully exploited this ambiguity, moving from thoughts-as-publicly-expressed to the 'I' thinking those thoughts at that moment (see p.39); but he was only establishing the coincidence of Thought 2 with Thought 1. Berkeley, however, seems both to inadvertently equate the two concepts of 'idea' *and* to suppose that his arguments have established this equation (see 3c) and d) above.) The form/content assimilation is conducive to the immaterialism and anti-scepticism he is trying to establish, but do his arguments justify it?

2) He says both that ideas are within the mind, *and* that they are distinct from, and outside, the mind. The ideas could, admittedly, be in the mind yet distinct from it, as eggs are distinct from the box that they are contained in, but he often seems to be saying that the ideas are also outside the mind. These positions on ideas sound inconsistent with one

Dr Samuel Johnson misunderstood Berkeley's position.

another, and either of them is also inconsistent with his contention that an idea is both the action of perceiving and the object being perceived. Possibly the inconsistency can be reconciled – if the mind in which the ideas inhere is God's, and the mind from which they are distinct is the human mind; although that should have been clarified.

3) Without God, and even with Him, Berkeley's subjective idealism seems solipsistic (see p.41). God causes me to have ideas (ideas that are in His mind), but what about other people's ideas and minds? How are they coordinated with mine so that we all agree on what we perceive and on what is happening? Wittgenstein says that solipsism 'coincides with pure realism'; that 'the self of solipsism shrinks to a point without extension, and there remains the reality co-ordinated with it' so that 'the subject does not belong to the world: rather, it is the limit of the world.' Arguably, Wittgenstein's solipsistic realism is similar to Berkeley's account of the self's relation to reality. But, given that, for Berkeley, I am not the only self, what about the other 'limits of the world'? Or should that be 'the limits of other worlds'? There would surely have to be more than one world for there to be limits of. A shared, communally perceived space seems to be outlawed by the *Principles*, the *Dialogues*, and also by *The New Theory of Vision*.

According to Berkeley, we have 'notions' of other selves. Yet we do not share their ideas, any more than one person can share someone else's dream. As in the film 'the Matrix' there is a false premise, which won't work: virtual reality can only accommodate one consciousness. Like the aliens in the Matrix, God must have logic-defying powers to arrange that all the virtual realities (ideas) are in step, so that, for instance, a woman's ideas of becoming pregnant coincide with the correspondent ideas of her foetus's father. (See also 7 [Minds] above.)

4) Isn't Berkeley going in a figure-of-eight to go in a straight line? His attempts to reconcile his theory with science (see above) are ludicrous. He seems surreptitiously to rely on the conventional beliefs (about the existence of objective space and a material world) even as he claims to repudiate them.

Worse, when challenged by Hylas, Philonous accepts the Genesis account of creation. It 'mentions the sun, moon, and stars, earth and sea, plants and animals: that all these do really exist, and were in the beginning created by God, I make no question ... Upon reading [it] therefore ... I understand that the several parts of the world became gradually perceivable to finite spirits, endowed with proper faculties; so that whoever such were present ['present' where?], they were in truth perceived by them.'

So God did in fact create the world and its objects, and God keeps these objects/ideas in existence – not for each person separately, like a sort of virtual reality, and not just creating ideas anew each time someone perceives, but in a public, permanent sort of way. In a public sort of space, too, or where would the finite spirits be 'present'?

Thus 'ideas' are indeed both within and 'without' [outside] the mind. And there are two sorts of ideas. Ideas A are *outside* the individual human mind – enduring, objective things which have 'a real existence' (Philonous invites Hylas to call ideas in this category 'things' if he wants to); they are 'archetypes', says Philonous, that God has created (and that presumably exist in His mind). Ideas B are *in* the individual human mind – subjective perceptions of the more objective Ideas A; 'ectypes' (as Philonous calls them) of the archetypes.

So, ultimately, Berkeley's idealist immaterialism seems to amount to dualistic Indirect Realism – to there being two types of stuff in the world, perceiving (minds and their ideas) and perceived (more permanent ideas, which are tantamount to physical things). There is 'a twofold state of things, the one ectypal or natural, the other archetypal and eternal' and a correspondence between the first and the second, as in Indirect Realism; even if 'things', for Berkeley, are less thingy than in usual dualisms.

5) The mental stuff that perceives is not communal or porous. What makes mental substances separate from one another must surely be the ideas (perceived by themselves and other mental substances) which constitute their own and one another's bodies. That fits oddly with idealism.

Key points

- Berkeley is an idealist (he believes that reality is fundamentally mental and immaterial).

- He argues that the so-called 'primary' qualities are as dependent on, and relative to us, as secondary ones.

- It's absurd, he says, to suppose that ideas are totally different to how they seem – that 'really' a sound, for instance, is not what we hear but what is potentially visible and touchable: a sound wave. With an idea, appearance *is* reality; seeming and being are one.

- Thus, only ideas and minds exist. One of the minds is God's. Ideas are continually caused in our minds and/or (Berkeley seems to vacillate on this) are kept in sustained existence, by His awareness of them.

- Berkeley says that the biblical account of Creation entails that our minds have ectypes of the archeyptes created by God which became perceivable to finite spirits, endowed with proper faculties. If so (and he doesn't fully endorse it), then we are left with the gap between what is and what seems – between things outside the mind and ideas in it, between what is perceived and the perceiving of it; precisely the gap that he was trying to close or deny.

- It is even possible to interpret Berkeley as postulating a world that, like Descartes' and Locke's, contains both physical and mental stuff. There remains room, in fact, for the scepticism that Berkeley was trying to scotch.

Chapter 6

David Hume (1711–76): Epistemology

D avid Hume is widely regarded as the greatest English-speaking philosopher ever. He was part of the Scottish Enlightenment, and yet, like the Romantics, he deflated the status of reason, and upgraded that of emotion. His subject was the 'science of man' which he considered 'the only solid foundation for the other sciences'. Opening the door to modernity, he treated humans as part of nature, rather than transcendent. In diagnosing the way we are driven by emotion, habit and unconscious mental mechanisms, he influenced Darwin, Freud, cognitive scientists and the Behaviourists. More immediately, Immanuel Kant wrote that Hume had awoken him from his 'dogmatic slumbers'.

David Hume was a leading figure of the Scottish Enlightenment, but his philosophy elevated the status of emotion and demoted that of reason.

FROM ARCH-SCEPTIC TO POST-SCEPTIC

In his extreme empiricism, Hume scandalizingly unsettled all our ordinary beliefs – the external world, the self, causation and induction all turn out to be dubious. But once considered an arch-sceptic, he is now seen as a 'post-sceptic': following the reasoning of Descartes, Locke and Berkeley to its logical conclusion, he shows it to be self-defeating and contradictory. A master of wit and paradox, he said that his reasoning compelled him to scepticism, but that his scepticism was most clearly demonstrated in his inability to believe it. His arguments are so convoluted and paradoxical that it is hard to know what he believed. 'Berkeley without God'? A phenomenalist? A common-sense dualist? Some philosophers (the self-styled New Humeans) variously claim that he held most of the beliefs he repudiated.

Similarly, in his moral philosophy (see Chapter 7), Hume urged that 'Reason is, and ought only to be the slave of the passions': It is emotion, not reason, that drives morality, and persuades us to move from *is* to *ought*. We feel sympathy, and this is our impetus to moral behaviour. By 'sympathy', however, Hume does not mean compassion, but instead an automatic sense of how those geographically and emotionally close to us are feeling, and a visceral discomfort if they are distressed. He thought that we need reason to extend our natural concern for ourselves and those we love into a more impartial concern for humankind in general.

LIFE

Hume was born on 26 April 1711 to a family of impoverished gentry with a small estate on the English-Scottish border. At the age of 12, he joined his brother at Edinburgh University, supposedly to read law, which he hated, but in reality secretly 'devouring' classical authors such as Cicero and Virgil. He never graduated but left university aged 15, and spent the next three years thinking and studying at home, during which time he lost his Calvinist faith and became, if not an atheist, which he always denied (it was scandalous at the time), agnostic at least and anti-religion (especially Catholicism). Struggling to find 'some new medium, by which truth might be establisht', and to think beyond all borders, brought him to the brink of giddy madness that he describes in *A Treatise of Human Nature* (1738), and perhaps beyond. Aged eighteen, he was struck down with an undiagnosed illness (perhaps depression) which had few physical symptoms, but which 'extinguished' his 'ardour', leaving him unable to think or write for nine months.

After briefly doing clerical work in Bristol, Hume spent several years living cheaply at Descartes' old college, La Flèche, where he had amiable arguments with the Jesuits, and wrote the *Treatise*. Its first two books *(Of the Understanding* and *Of the Passions)* were published anonymously in 1739, and the third, *Of Morals*, in 1740, along with an anonymous *Abstract* summarizing Book 1. Although Hume had 'castrated' it of 'its nobler parts', such as the attack on miracles, so as to 'give as little offence as possible', the *Treatise* was brilliant, daring, iconoclastic, and he expected it to at least 'excite a murmur among the zealots'. He was mortified when, to scanty, uncomprehending reviews, it 'fell dead-born from the press'.

For the next few years Hume wrote well-received essays, briefly served as tutor to the mad Marquis of Annandale, and was secretary to General St Clair, accompanying him to the courts of Vienna and Turin, and on an absurd maritime invasion of Brittany. His applications for a chair at the University of Edinburgh (1745), and of Glasgow (1751), were turned down – it wasn't only Boswell who considered him 'the great infidel'. His publisher was threatened with legal action for some of Hume's essays, which were then suppressed. This didn't stop him writing controversially on religion. *The Natural History of Religion* appeared in 1757 as one of the *Four Dissertations*, and he arranged for *Dialogues Concerning Natural Religion* to be published posthumously by his nephew. All his works are proscribed in the Catholic index of forbidden books.

As a youth, Hume spent his free time reading the works of classical writers like Cicero.

Denis Diderot was a leading figure of the Enlightenment and one of the many French philosophers Hume met in Paris.

Hume at last won fame as a historian, and became much better known for his six-volume history of England (published between 1754 and 1762) than for his philosophical *Enquiry concerning Human Understanding* (1748) and *Enquiry concerning the Principles of Morals* (1751), which are sometimes considered his greatest works. The *Enquiries* include previously 'castrated' material on miracles, and omit the topic of personal identity, which Hume had confessed himself baffled by in the *Treatise's* Appendix. Scholars heatedly divide over whether he was rearticulating or replacing the *Treatise*, and how far he was being purely strategic in disparaging 'that juvenile work'. Admittedly it was the only one he didn't revise in old age.

In 1763, Hume spent three years in Paris as private secretary to the English ambassador, and was wonderfully feted at the salons, meeting Enlightenment figures like Diderot, d'Alembert and Holbach, and the beautiful Comtesse de Boufflers. In 1766 he returned to England with Jean-Jacques Rousseau, whom at first Hume loved, but who predictably turned paranoid, their quarrel becoming a *cause célèbre*.

In 1775, Hume became seriously ill, probably with liver cancer. He was perfectly sanguine about death (to Dr Johnson's fury when Boswell reported this), still unrepentantly irreligious, and he continued to be witty and eloquent until the end.

HUME'S EPISTEMOLOGY

Hume wanted to be a Newton of the mind. He was perhaps the first philosopher before Kant to ask what properties the human mind must have in order for us to think, feel and act as we do, and to consider human behaviour as part of nature, and therefore within the scope of empirical science. Considering 'the essence of the mind [to be] equally unknown to us with that of external bodies', he tries to discover and itemize the forces that drive it, as Newton had charted the laws of motion in the physical world. He is extending Descartes' 'mechanical philosophy'. Instead of exempting the human mind from causal forces – Descartes claims that we have free will to assent (or not) to the truth and accuracy of our ideas – Hume seeks to classify its automatic currents of association. According to Descartes, we should reject any beliefs that lack rational justification. For Hume, there are no rational grounds for believing much of what we believe, but that doesn't mean we believe it irrationally. The non-rational laws of our human nature make us think in certain ways.

Mental furniture

Like Descartes, Locke and Berkeley, Hume starts out from Indirect Realism. 'Nothing is ever present to the mind but perceptions,' he says, but he calls them 'impressions' to distinguish them from 'ideas'.

1) Impressions and ideas.
   a) He explains that he has restored 'idea' to the original meaning 'from which Mr Locke had perverted it, in making it stand for all our perceptions'. He uses the term 'impressions' for the immediate 'lively' perceptions that fleetingly strike us (either sensory experiences (for example colours, tastes, shapes) or 'reflexions'– our 'inner' reactions to sensory experience (for example desire or aversion)). He uses 'idea' for the fainter but more permanent copy of an impression that is retained as a concept.
   b) Just as impressions are converted into ideas, so ideas 'return upon the soul' to produce new impressions. An impression of discomfort co-occurring with an impression of coldness produces ideas of each, which in turn produce an inner impression of aversion towards such ideas, and towards repeating the impressions that caused them.

impression $- - - - - - - >$ idea $- - - - - - >$ impression

c) All our knowledge consists of ideas derived from sense impressions. You can't have an idea of scarlet, for instance, if you lack the requisite sense (sight), or lack the requisite experience (seeing something scarlet) so as to have an impression of scarlet in the first place. (Here he naughtily presupposes an external world.)

But Hume supplies a counterexample to his theory. If someone is presented with a range of blues graduating from very light to very dark, with one shade missing, 'he will perceive a blank' and be aware of 'a greater distance in that place between the contiguous colours than in any other'. Hume may be wrong as to the confident recognition of a precise missing shade, but perhaps the principle is right – painters, when mixing their palettes, probably have some sort of idea of some intermediate colour that they've had no impression of. Even so, Hume relies too much on a 'picture' notion of impressions and ideas.

d) He concedes that we are able to form a 'relative idea' of external objects, 'without pretending [claiming] to comprehend them'. Some New Humeans argue that the term 'relative idea' (sometimes used by Hume, and also by Locke and Berkeley) offers the Indirect Realist a way out from the solipsistic corral of the mind. Locke, for instance, says that, thanks to a 'relative idea superadded to' our perceptions, 'the mind frames the correlative idea of a support [of the qualities perceived].'

e) The impressions from which we derive ideas do not have to be our own direct impressions. Historians (like Hume himself) can glean impressions of the past from their impressions of the texts (primary sources) which record the impressions had by, for instance, Caesar of crossing the Rubicon (one of Hume's examples).

f) Imagination and memory extend our mental furniture:

   i) We can, in imagination, join ideas as we wish (for example gold + mountain = golden mountain). The idea of God comes from 'augmenting, without limit, those qualities of goodness and wisdom' which we find in ourselves and others.

   ii) Memory is 'intermediate betwixt an impression and an idea'. Hume assumes memory is an exact copier – except where it's defective! He (unconvincingly) says that, although we can imagine events that didn't happen, such imaginings are 'fainter and more obscure' than real memories.

2) There are three principles which prompt us to move from one idea to another (these are the mental counterpart to Newton's laws of motion): resemblance, contiguity, cause and effect. (A portrait leads our thoughts to the absent friend represented in the portrait, as does the sight of his son; mention of one apartment in a building leads to speculation about the others; if we see, or think of, a wound, we automatically imagine the resulting pain.)

Our minds, then, perform operations and connections of which we are unaware, carrying us from one idea to another 'by a gentle and insensible movement'. It is less that *we* make associations than that they are *made for us* by 'the current of nature'. Hume is a precursor of the computer model of mind – he suggests that the mind is more a set of activities than of contents, and that in many cases we don't have introspective access to these (the hardware runs the software). He probably also influenced Freud's theories of the unknown pulleys in the mind (libido, the Oedipus complex, defence mechanisms, the 'dream-work').

Freud's theories of the unknown pulleys in the mind likely owed much to the influence of Hume.

He says, however, that we are not *compelled* to make associations; the principles he diagnoses do not constitute 'an inseparable connexion'. They are, however, prompted by 'a kind of attraction' – 'a gentle force, which commonly prevails', and is 'guided by some universal principles, which render it, in some measure, uniform with itself in all times and places'.

3) Hume's Fork: the objects of human enquiry divide – exclusively – into relations of ideas and matters of fact.
   a) Relations of ideas: 'every affirmation which is either intuitively or demonstratively certain', and 'discoverable by the mere operation of thought, without dependence on what is anywhere existent in the universe.' For example geometry, algebra, and arithmetic.
   b) Matters of fact: 'The contrary of every matter of fact is still possible; because it can never imply a contradiction, and is conceived by the mind with the same facility and distinctness, as if ever so conformable to reality.' For example, it is possible to envisage the sun not rising tomorrow, and we do so without contradicting ourselves.

Belief

Belief 'depends not on the will, nor can be commanded at pleasure'. We think about plenty of things that we don't believe in. When we do believe them, we don't add to, subtract from, or in any way alter, our original idea of them. What is altered is the vividness of how we conceive the idea, which becomes 'more strong and lively'. Belief, then, is adverbial – and involuntary and visceral. 'When I am convinc'd of any principle, 'tis only an idea, which strikes more strongly upon me,' Hume says.

It could be objected that many of our beliefs are dormant, rather than palpable or consciously entertained; some are unconscious and unadmitted to. Also, we often have less 'vivacious' conceptions of what we do believe in than of a fantasy or an imaginary scenario. Historical fiction often produces livelier ideas than when we read historical facts.

Knowledge

The belief that Hume is apparently forced to have is the empiricist one that genuine knowledge, since it depends on prior sense experience, must ultimately be derivable from impressions. Any ideas claimed to be true must be traceable back to impressions (not necessarily our own ones), or to relations between ideas, as in maths; otherwise they are illegitimate. In the *Enquiry*, he famously exhorts us to 'run over libraries' and examine each book for whether it contains either 'experimental reasoning concerning matter of fact and existence' or abstract mathematical reasoning. If not, 'Commit it then to the flames: for it can contain nothing but sophistry and illusion'.

This wreaking of 'havoc', as Hume gleefully puts it, is what inspired A.J. Ayer and other Logical Positivists in the 20th century with their pronouncement that metaphysics, ethics, aesthetics, and anything else impossible to empirically verify are meaningless. In fact Hume is an infinitely more nuanced, complex, sensitive thinker than they are.

The external world

'Impression' has a metaphorical implication – that the mind, like soft wax, is imprinted with the stamp of a signet ring. Some of the Stoics, whom we know Hume had read, used precisely that metaphor to describe how we perceive. But they were taking for granted the existence of material objects, as did Locke, for all his proclaimed empiricism. Hume doesn't always keep within his professed limits (impressions and ideas), but won't resort to God as guarantor of objectivity. (Mysteriously [see p.120], he does say, 'The farthest we can go towards a conception of external objects, when suppos'd *specifically* different from our perceptions, is to form a relative idea of them, without pretending to comprehend the related objects.')

1) Since we cannot get outside our perceptions, how are we to establish that there is an external world of substances that exist continuously, and independent of us?
   a) Do we have an impression of substance? No. 'If [substance] be perceiv'd by the eyes, it must be a colour; if by the ears, a sound; if by the palate, a taste.' Nor is it derived from an impression of

reflection (it isn't a sensation or emotion). Therefore, we have no idea of substance other than the impressions we have of a collection of particular qualities; that is all 'substance' can mean.

b) Nor can our senses give us the 'notion' (Hume borrows Berkeley's weasel word) of the continued existence of impressions once they cease to appear to the senses.

c) Nor do the senses 'offer ... their impressions' of the independent existence of what they perceive. 'A single perception can never produce the idea of a double existence, but by some inference either of the reason or imagination.' 'Double existence' must mean the existence both of the perception and what it is putatively a perception *of* (some physical thing in the external world). A perception doesn't convey anything beyond the perception itself.

2) How are we to differentiate the impressions of our own bodies from the rest of the impressions we're having?

a) It is 'absurd ... to imagine the senses can ever distinguish betwixt ourselves and external objects'. For: 'every impression, external and internal, passions, affections, sensations, pains and pleasures, are originally on the same footing; and ... whatever other differences we may observe among them, they appear, all of them in their true colours, as impressions or perceptions.' Since they are all 'known to us by consciousness, they must necessarily appear in every particular what they are, and be what they appear.'

b) It could be said that our own body 'evidently' belongs to us; 'and as several impressions appear exterior to it, we suppose them also exterior to ourselves. The paper on which I write at present, is beyond my hand. The table is beyond the paper. The walls of the chamber beyond the table. And in casting my eye towards the window, I perceive a great extent of fields and buildings beyond my chamber.' Yet 'properly speaking, 'tis not our body we perceive, when we regard our limbs and members, but certain impressions, which enter by the senses'. My 'body' is as much a series of perceptions as anything else. 'The mind has never anything present to it but the perceptions, and cannot possibly reach any experience of their connexion with objects'.

3) Hume invokes the secondary quality distinction: Sounds, tastes and smells don't occupy space, and therefore can't appear to us 'as situated externally to the body'.

4) Anyway, we have no impression of space ('outness'); a Berkeleian point.

Why, then, do we imagine that things exist external to, and independent of, us? Because there is 'constancy' and 'coherence' in the way we experience certain groups of impressions. Like a galley put in motion by rowing, the imagination, when 'set into any train of thinking' tends to continue in it, even with no new input. Gaps between perceptions are thus glided over. Hume is full of smooth transitions.

Self and personal identity

Applying the impression test to the self is also devastating. Since Hume has made the body simply a series of impressions that are on a par with

The imagination is like a galley in motion – it tends to continue on its path, even without new inputs, and gaps are easily glided over.

Hume saw the mind as a theatre, where perceptions appear, mingle and disappear like actors.

the impressions supposedly outside it, he would seem to be cast back on a Cartesian self that is having these interchangeable impressions. But, inevitably, although we *seem* to have an idea of the self, we don't really count as having that idea because there is no impression from which to derive it. Some philosophers, Hume agrees, 'imagine we are every moment intimately conscious of what we call our SELF'; for his part, however, 'when I enter most intimately into what I call *myself*, I always stumble upon some particular perception or other, of heat or cold, light or shade, love or hatred, pain or pleasure. I never can catch *myself* at any time without a perception, and never can observe any thing but the perception.' In fact, says Hume, if your mind were reduced to a lower grade of existence than an oyster's, and had only one perception, you would still have no coherent sense of self or be able to perceive anything more than that one perception.

The mind, says Hume, 'is a kind of theatre, where several perceptions successively make their appearance; pass, re-pass, glide away, and mingle in an infinite variety of postures and situations.' It has neither unity at any one moment, nor identity over time. Don't, he tells the reader, be misled by the theatre simile. The 'successive perceptions' do not occur *in* the mind; they constitute it. 'Ourself, independent of the perception of every other object, is in reality nothing.' Or 'it' is 'a bundle of perceptions', or something like 'a republic or commonwealth', the members of which are united by 'reciprocal ties of government and subordination'.

One might wonder what ties the bundle together, or how the 'subordination' works, especially as Hume declares the will to be 'nothing but' the 'internal impression we feel and are conscious of, when we knowingly give rise to any new motion of our body, or new perception of our mind'. However, he clearly considers the will to be more than a mere impression (elsewhere he mentions its 'influencing motives'.)

So why do we think we have an idea of self? Although there is no 'real bond' among our perceptions, the imagination's tendency smoothly to merge discrete objects prompts us to 'feign' (pretend) the continued existence of what we perceive in ourselves so that we 'run into the notion of a *soul*, and *self* and *substance*'. As usual, it sounds as if we are compelled to think the way we do, yet are somehow fraudulent as well.

But who is the 'we' that is feigning, imagining, compelled? Hume's treatment of the emotions in *Treatise* Book 2 relies on there being a self to which our passions of pride or humility refer the attributes, skills, possessions and actions that merit either emotion; although opposites, they both have 'the same OBJECT'. Discussing love of fame, he says that 'the idea, or rather impression of ourselves is always intimately present with us, and that our consciousness gives us [a] lively . . . conception of our own person.' Admittedly, he does make a distinction between personal identity 'as it regards our thought and imagination', and as it regards our emotions and self-concern, but does that help to absolve him from contradiction? And surely, his entire project is to analyse the mind, considered as a discrete entity, and how it works. In the Appendix, Hume confesses that his discussion of personal identity has become embroiled in a 'labyrinth', and that he cannot render it consistent.

Causation

Are we then forever stuck in our current set of impressions? Hume seems to offer a way out. If we believe in causation, that enables us to infer from the present to the past, and from here to elsewhere. From finding a

Hume was said to look more like a 'turtle-eating alderman' than 'a refined philosopher'.

HUME'S EPITAPH

On Hume's tomb in Edinburgh is written:

'Within this circular Idea
Called vulgarly a Tomb
The Impressions and Ideas rest
That constituted Hume.'

watch on a desert island, I conclude that some human has been there; my reason for thinking my friend is in France is that I receive a letter from him, and remember his declared intentions.

There is no one quality, Hume points out, which all causes have in common. Rather, causation is a complex idea of:

1) Contiguity (the cause closely touching on the effect);

2) Priority of time (the cause occurring before the effect);

3) Constant conjunction (a certain type of 'object' is invariably followed by another type of 'object');

4) Necessary connection (one type of 'object' not only always follows another type, but necessarily follows it. There is a necessary connection between cause and effect.)

A PRIORI KNOWLEDGE

A priori knowledge is knowledge that we have without experience, and that no amount of experience can disprove. Mathematical knowledge is a priori. Obviously we do not emerge from the womb knowing that 2 + 2 = 4, but, as Plato demonstrated in his dialogue *Meno*, even someone ignorant of maths and geometry can, if asked clear questions about the properties of squares, answer correctly, as if they already have (innate) knowledge. *A posteriori* knowledge, on the other hand, is knowledge that we acquire through our own or other people's experience.

We have impressions from which to derive the first three ideas, but do we have an impression of necessary connection?

Where does the idea of causation come from?

The idea of causation is not known a priori. 'From the first appearance of an object, we never can conjecture what effect will result from it.' And 'there is nothing in any object, consider'd in itself, which can afford us a reason for drawing a conclusion beyond it.' Adam (the first man) could not have guessed that water would drown him; a child has to learn the effects of fire; and who could have anticipated the effects of gun powder when ignited? Do we, then, get the idea of causation through experience (*a posteriori*)? Well, we have experience of causes being contiguous to effects, and preceding them, and the two being constantly conjoined (we see one billiard ball strike another, and that the struck ball immediately moves). But what about the fourth idea that composes the complex idea of causation – the idea of necessary connection? Do we perhaps get it:

1) From an impression of external power, which we acquire when we will movements such as raising our arms? (This is what Locke thought.) No, because:

The thousandth time we observe one billiard ball striking another adds nothing to our first observation, so where does our impression of necessary connection come from?

a) bodily movement 'follows upon the command of our will', but how 'the most refined thought is able to actuate the grossest matter' is totally mysterious.

b) different organs depend, to a greater (tongue and fingers), lesser (bowels), or no (heart) extent, on the will. In each case, we learn this from experience, just as we do causes and effects outside the body. Someone newly struck with paralysis continues for a time to feel they can move their limbs, and has to get used to not being able to do so. (We also learn, or rather are taught, to control our bladders and bowels; again with absolutely no sense of how we acquire this control.)

c) Although knowledge of anatomy (which most people don't have) informs us about causal links between nerves, muscles and 'animal spirits', we can't feel each of the linking events, only the final outcome. Hume's point, also made by Malebranche, remains valid, however much neurological and anatomical knowledge becomes available. Try to intercept the act of willing your finger to bend, and it bending. 'Here the mind wills a certain event: Immediately another event, unknown to ourselves, and totally different from the one intended, is produced: This event produces another, equally unknown: Till at last, through a long succession, the desired event is produced.'

2) From an impression of internal power, which we gain when we 'raise up a new idea', contemplate and examine, then dismiss it? No, because:

a) Once again, it is mysterious how on earth this happens. 'This is a real creation; a production of something out of nothing', and we haven't a clue how we effect it.

b) The mind has limited control over itself, less over emotions than over ideas.

c) Such self-command as we do have 'is very different at different times', diminished due to illness, tiredness, hunger.

The missing impression of necessary connection

So the idea of necessary connection is derived neither from an impression of external power, nor from an impression of internal power. And, as with any idea, if it is not derived from some original impression, then we are not justified in holding it. But we do. We see the man stumble on the cliff edge, and we gasp in horrified anticipation. How is it that we 'know' that he will inevitably fall?

The first time we observe a causal sequence (A followed by B), we won't expect B to follow A (says Hume). After repeatedly observing that type of causal sequence, we do expect that. Yet the invariable observations 'can only multiply, but not enlarge the objects of our mind'. The first time we witness the conjunction of events/objects is no different from the next and the next; each is just a repetition of the same kind of impressions we've already had. If one instance of cause and effect won't show us necessity, then many such instances don't either. Yet we 'find' ourselves ineluctably inferring that the effect will follow, 'even tho' there be no reason to determine us to that transition'.

Hume constantly stresses the automaticity of our thinking, the Newton-like mental forces that drive our thoughts, and that belief is a sort of sentiment, more visceral than rational. Imagination, twinned with habit, makes us 'draw, from a thousand instances, an inference which we are not able to draw from one instance, that is, in no respect, different from them'. To do so is unavoidable. 'The power and necessity . . . are consequently qualities of perceptions, not of objects, are internally felt by the soul, and not perceiv'd externally in bodies.' And so, in a reversal of what might be expected, 'the necessary connexion depends on the inference, instead of the inference's depending on the necessary connexion.'

Could there be necessary connection after all?

This of course leaves open the possibility that, as well as the sense of necessity we feel (having extrapolated it from observing constant conjunctions), there actually *is* necessity in those constant conjunctions themselves. Hume could (as some New Humeans contest) believe that despite the fact that our inability to observe necessary connections prohibits us from justifiably postulating them, they do nonetheless exist. Maybe he conveys and implies, rather than explicitly argues, this.

As so often, he is ambiguous. On the one hand, he writes that 'upon the whole, necessity is something, that exists in the mind', and is nothing more than the automatic movement of thought from 'causes' to 'effects' 'according to their experienc'd union'. On the other hand, he says, 'It is universally allowed that matter in all its operations, is actuated by a necessary force'. In which case, when we 'always presume' that 'secret powers' must inhabit the causal object/event, we are right – even if we cannot know the nature of these powers.

In both the *Treatise* and the *Enquiry* he nominates 'cause and effect' (along with resemblance and contiguity) as one of the three 'principles of connexion' that shift us from one idea to another. And the associations we mechanically make (or that are made for us by 'the current of nature') necessarily cause us to (unjustifiably) believe in causal necessity. So there are necessary connections in our minds, if not in the material world; although his treatment of 'liberty and necessity' (free will and determinism) is, inevitably, ambiguous.

We may, then, be projecting outwards an impression of what is there anyway but is beyond the boundaries of our experience, beyond what we can have impressions of. Sometimes Hume seems to imply that behind the wall of justifiable knowledge is almost certainly the reality that we

---

HUME ON LIBERTY AND NECESSITY

To dispute whether an action is caused or freely done is, says Hume, just a matter of words. In practice we agree that there is no such thing as chance in the natural world, and similarly, whatever we may say, we apply the same principles when considering human actions. We predict that a dropped purse will not remain untouched, just as we predict that it will not fly. Explicitly or not, we believe that punishment and reward cause children, and people generally, to behave better, because it modifies their expectations and desires. Those who insist on free will are in effect expecting desires to be uncaused and random, as the madman's appear to be. What counts as freedom, says Hume, is being able to do what we want to do, even though our wants themselves are not under our control. His use of the term 'liberty', which can be ambiguous between moral, psychological and political freedom, makes this argument more persuasive than if he had used 'free will'.

DEFINITIONS OF CAUSE

Hume offers two definitions of cause, and there is incessant argument about whether or not he considers them synonymous.

1) 'An object precedent and contiguous to another, and where all the objects resembling the former are plac'd in like relations of precedency and contiguity to those objects, that resemble the latter.'

2) 'A cause is an object precedent and contiguous to another, and so united with it, that the idea of the one determines the mind to form the idea of the other, and the impression of the one to form a more lively idea of the other.'

unjustifiably assume. Or we may be projecting a fabricated, non-sensed and non-existent necessity onto the external world. (The unacknowledged projector lurks, today, in physicalist theories of mind (see pages 104, 127)).

But is Hume entitled to say either that there are, or are not, necessary connexions, either inside or outside the mind, or both? Is he consistent in treating the mind, as Indirect Realists do – as if, in its own occult extrasensory realm, it receives inputs from an external world and puts its own spin on them; is able to conjure up an illusion of 'necessary connections' that it never actually observes. Surely his whole point is that the mind is not exempt from natural laws, is itself another natural phenomenon, which contains (or consists of) Newton-like forces. How come there are 'internal' necessary connections that he (perhaps) denies to other external natural phenomena, and that he certainly claims we cannot perceive between material objects?

The problem of induction

Whatever the pros and cons of Hume's view on causation, he is revolutionary in showing how wrong we (rationally) are to trust induction (the inference of a general law from the observation of many particular but recurring instances). Induction is the basis of science, which aims to discover the laws of nature, and also of practical everyday

You don't know the 'secret powers' of bread, so, just because it has sated your hunger in the past, why should it do so in the future?

life. We all 'know' that the sun will rise tomorrow. 'Know?' demands Hume. Just because there have so far been invariable constant conjunctions (the sun setting in the evening and rising in the morning), what in either reason or experience assures us that those constant conjunctions will continue to be invariable? What guarantees that 'the future will be conformable to the past'? To argue that the future will be like the past because it always has been is 'taking that for granted, which is the very point in question'; it is to argue in a circle.

You may insist that bread has always nourished you, Hume says, but 'your appeal to past experience decides nothing in the present case'. There is 'no known connexion between [a loaf's] sensible qualities and [its] secret powers'. Why assume that, because certain sensible qualities are now, and have always been, attended with the power to nourish, they always will be?

Ah, you might say, those secret powers are secret no longer. We now know that bread contains carbohydrates (organic compounds containing hydrogen and oxygen that typically can be broken down to release energy in the body). Yes, but why do these carbohydrate biomolecules occur? How are they able to be broken down? And why does that decomposition create energy? However far down you go, the connection between disparate things and events remains unnecessary and unknown. Scientific discovery 'only staves off our ignorance a little longer', and it will never supply an impression of necessary connection.

The problem of induction remains, and purported solutions to it by philosophers and scientists fail: what guarantees that, in future, causes and effects that have thus far reliably occurred will continue to do so? There is no point invoking the laws of nature. Only the existence of a divine law-giver would justify us in postulating perennial laws rather than merely past regularities.

But try *not* assuming that there are necessary connections between certain events, and that there aren't reliable natural laws. How are you going to manage to do that? Are you going to live recklessly ('I think I'll just walk out of the window of this six-storey building. After all, there is no infallible certainty that I'll fall') or neurotically ('I daren't walk across the room because it's quite conceivable that the floor will collapse')? Our beliefs are visceral and are not based on reason, says Hume. Luckily for us, they are compelled and compulsive.

The compulsiveness of induction also explains prejudice, which is precisely an example of how, if we have habitually observed objects A and B occurring together, then, on observing A (or similar), we expect B also. Thanks to habit, the imagination, 'passes from' one object to another 'by a natural transition'. Thus 'men form general rules, and allow them to influence their judgement, even contrary to present observation and experience'.

So, how sceptical *is* Hume?

He describes himself as only 'a mitigated sceptic', and says that his scepticism is uneven, he can't sustain it, that perhaps he shows it most clearly by his very inability to live and practise it. Sometimes 'the *intense* view of these manifold contradictions and imperfections in human reason has so wrought upon me, and heated my brain that . . . I begin to fancy myself . . . inviron'd with the deepest darkness', but nature herself dispels these clouds and 'cures me of this philosophical melancholy and delirium'. The intensity of thought slackens, and he goes out, dines, plays backgammon and is 'merry with my friends', so that when he returns, these speculations appear simply 'cold, and strain'd, and ridiculous'.

Although, as a philosopher, he doubts causation, induction, the external world, the self, 'as an agent, I am quite satisfied' about them. 'Thus the sceptic still continues to reason and believe even though he asserts that he cannot defend his reason by reason . . . Nature has not left this to his choice'.

Hume, heralding modernity, shows that reason is not our essence – that, as Schopenhauer would say, 'we are not winged cherubs without a body'. Our beliefs are species-specific, not non-perspectival and absolute. Descartes' project for a purely objective conception of the world is impossible. 'Reason can never satisfy us' of our common-sense beliefs, but if we cannot rationally justify them, 'the current of nature', of which we are part, forces us simultaneously to believe and disbelieve them. 'We may well ask, What causes induce us to believe in the existence of body? but 'tis in vain to ask, Whether there be body or not? That is a point, which we must take for granted in all our reasonings.' If (abstract) reasoning compels us to be sceptics, (practical) reasoning forces us not to be.

Using a metaphor that wonderfully accords with his own comfortable corpulence, he says belief tends not to be whole-hearted when 'the posture of the mind is uneasy' or 'forc'd and unnatural': it has to be 'founded on something natural and easy'. Strained philosophical (as opposed to comfy commonsensical) belief is like the clear-sighted bleakness of depression – rational yet diseased and unnatural. Whereas the absurd unmerited optimism which makes us believe in, and feel, the goodness of life is irrational, but healthy and normal.

Hume anticipated the theory of evolution when he saw reason as a mechanical power and an important survival mechanism.

Hume's double-speak

Hume uses 'reason' in at least two different senses. 'To consider the matter aright, reason is nothing but a wonderful and unintelligible instinct in our souls, which carries us along a certain train of ideas'. It (at least in the case of 'experimental reasoning') is a 'mechanical power' that we 'possess in common with the beasts', and that 'acts on us' to make us avoid dangers. Anticipating evolutionary theory, he makes reason just another useful survival mechanism.

But he also uses 'reason' in its more traditional sense , as a faculty superior to the beasts', although saying it is too 'slow in its operations' for our survival to 'be trusted to [its] fallacious deductions', whereas 'some instinct or mechanical tendency' may work 'infallibly'. It is just as well that we are guided not by reason but by custom and imagination. Reason, then, is something distinct from the natural, and potentially counterproductive to it; is, indeed, often the awkward origin of all the problems and puzzles he is drawing attention to.

Hume both subsumes the human mind in the natural world and elevates it above nature. The periscope of reason seems to poke up above what we actually believe and do, enabling him to say we have no reason to believe in what we believe in (even though we have to believe it).

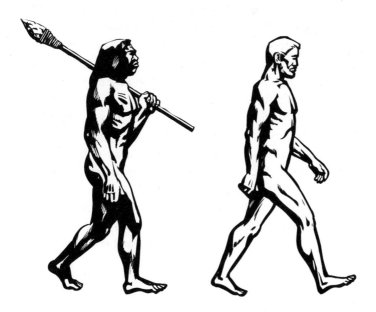

Still more duplicitous is the advantage he takes of 'seem'. When he says that 'all events seem entirely loose and separate', that 'seem' must surely just be a 'seem' of abstract reason rather than a sensorily experienced seeming. For he keeps telling us that our minds automatically and unconsciously (with the momentum of gliding galleys) obliterate the gaps between things and events so that they constantly *seem* continuous (even while reason demonstrates that they are not). Whenever Hume says that we cannot avoid believing or doing x, or that y is 'nothing but z', we should be wary.

Where are we?

'Where am I, or what?' Hume asks in his philosophical delirium. If the existence of the external world is so dubious, where is everything? Perhaps he is not required to account for the causes of impressions, or the location of the mind. He is after all doing 'the science of man', not of the world; writing epistemology rather than metaphysics. 'When we see, that we have arrived at the utmost extent of human reason, we sit down contented; though we be perfectly satisfied in the main of our ignorance, and perceive that we can give no reason for our most general and refined principles, beside our experience of their reality.' As he says, 'an object can exist, and yet be no where [sic]: and I assert, that this is not only possible, but that the greatest part of beings do and must exist after this manner.'

But if we don't experience the mechanisms that makes us experience, and our conscious beliefs are the result of unconscious processes which happen as if behind the (perceivable) scenes, then how does he himself get to have ideas of the necessary connections occurring in the mind – or in fact of any of the associational mechanisms that he postulates? How could he have impressions of mental connections, in either his own mind or anyone else's? Yet if he hasn't had such impressions of impressions, then his writings about them surely count as those works of 'sophistry and illusion' that he urges us to hurl into the fire.

Hume's paradoxes are infuriating but rich, ingenious and seminal. Why should we expect this great 18th-century philosopher to have the pettifogging consistency of today's analytical philosophers?

Key points

- Hume was the first philosopher to ask what the properties the human mind must have in order for us to think, feel and act as we do, and to consider human behaviour as part of nature.

- Instead of exempting the human mind from causal forces, Hume seeks to classify its automatic currents of association.

- All our knowledge consists of ideas derived from sense impressions. There are three principles which prompt us to move from one idea to another: resemblance, contiguity, cause and effect.

- Although outlining causal forces in the mind, he casts doubt on whether causation, in the sense we normally mean it, actually occurs.

- Nonetheless we believe in causation, because it is useful for us to do so.

- Hume also shows how wrong we are to trust induction – the inference of a general law from the observation of many particular but recurring instances. What guarantees that 'the future will be conformable to the past'?

- Belief is just an easeful way of conceiving an idea.

- For Hume, there are no rational grounds for believing much of what we believe, but that doesn't mean we believe it irrationally.

Chapter 7

David Hume (1711–76): Moral Philosophy

We might expect Hume to do the same demolition job on morality as he does on causation, the external world and the self – perhaps even to adopt Moral Nihilism (the view that morality is a fiction), or to take the line of 20th-century philosopher John Mackie and deny that there could be objective moral values, since if there were, they would be uniquely weird facts in the fabric of the world. After all, from what (Humean) impression could we derive our ideas of moral value?

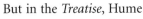

Moral Rationalists like William Wollaston claimed that moral values were absolute.

But in the *Treatise*, Hume declares that morality affects us so much that it 'can never be a chimera'. And the *Enquiry* opens by declaring that only people who want to seem clever ever claim to believe that there are no moral distinctions. Who, he asks, could genuinely think all characters and actions to be equally likeable and commendable? Everyone 'must often be touched with the images of Right and Wrong.'

Is Hume being uncharacteristically lenient, even evasive, in the case of morality? In discussing our knowledge, he is stringently empirical, not satisfied merely to observe what we do, think and feel, but questioning its ultimate validity; actually saying that we only 'imagine' that we feel some of the things we feel. But perhaps he is accepting the institution of morality as it is, and only seeking 'the true origin of morals' as a social phenomenon. Does he, like Aristotle, examine what are already accepted as virtues and vices, or does he probe deeper?

> Moral Subjectivism is like Emotivism in making morality a matter of feeling. But while Emotivists hold that a moral statement ('Torture is wrong') is merely expressing approval/disapproval (perhaps as a form of persuasion), Subjectivists generally hold that a moral statement really *is* a statement (not an exclamation): what it states is the speaker's feelings ('I approve/disapprove…').

Hume's moral philosophy is variously interpreted, but his arguments at least converge in demoting reason in favour of sentiment. He was concerned to oppose the contemporary Moral Rationalists (Ralph Cudworth, William Wollaston, Samuel Clarke) who claimed that moral values are God-ordained and absolute, and moral propositions as objectively true (when true) as mathematical ones are. He was supporting the Sentimentalist approach of Francis Hutcheson and Lord Shaftesbury, which invokes feeling and taste as constituting the 'moral sense'. But his complex arguments present a far more nuanced account of morality than either faction, and ultimately he invokes reason to mitigate the bias inherent in emotion.

IS AND OUGHT

In a famous passage in the *Treatise*, Hume remarks that thinkers in all the moral systems he has encountered tend to engage in the ordinary sort of reasoning and establishing of facts, until suddenly he is 'surpriz'd to find' that, instead of 'is' and 'is not', all their propositions contain 'ought' and 'ought not'. An 'imperceptible' shift has occurred to a 'new relation' which needs to be explained. To point this out, Hume declares, is to 'subvert all the vulgar systems of morality, and let us see, that the distinction of vice and virtue is not founded merely on the relations of objects, nor is perceiv'd by reason'.

Some 20th-century philosophers argue that he is proposing a new way of doing moral philosophy, one of a range of positions now called Non-cognitivism. These hold that moral statements are not in fact statements at all, so that when we say an action or attribute is good or bad, we are either expressing approval (or disapproval) towards it (Emotivism), or issuing a disguised command or recommendation that it be (or not be) done or adopted (Prescriptivism). Exclamations and commands are incapable of being true or false. There are no moral facts, we cannot have moral knowledge. Both these and other sorts of Moral Non-cognitivist positions take Hume to be indicating a gap between is and ought that involves an aeroplane take-off from descriptive to a quite different sort of discourse.

Moral impressions

Certainly Hume may have Non-cognitivist inclinations, but he often talks as if moral statements are indeed factual, though not

Are the terms 'virtuous' and 'vicious' merely expressions of approval or disapproval?

factual in the way we assume. In the passage just preceding the is-ought paragraph, he invites the reader to consider any action considered vicious – deliberate murder, for instance. What impression of vice do you have? he asks. However you examine the action, no 'vice' is perceptible by sight, hearing, smell, touch or taste. All you can find are emotions, motives, willings, thoughts (presumably of the murderer and her victim). Only when you 'turn your reflexion into your own breast' do you find an impression – the feeling 'which arises in you' of disapproval towards the action. Thus when you declare an action or person to be vicious, 'you mean nothing, but that from the constitution of your nature you have a feeling or sentiment of blame from the contemplation of it'.

This sounds as if Hume is saying that moral values are a question of purely individual taste and feeling, and indeed many consider him to hold a Subjectivist position. In a way he *is* talking about individual taste, but, significantly, he is saying that your (the reader's) visceral reaction is 'an internal sense or feeling, which nature has made universal in the whole species'. So the feeling is not just arbitrary and up to personal whim; it is objective, not in a scientific sense, but in a psychological and social one. Morality is not a 'queer fact' in the world's fabric (à la Mackie) but a fact about human feelings. For an action, attribute or person to be praiseworthy or blameable is not (*pace* the Moral Rationalists) the same as for it to be true or false. Feelings are not the sort of things that agree or disagree with reality, they themselves are 'original facts and realities'.

Vice and virtue do not 'antecedently exist' as 'eternal fitnesses and unfitnesses' to reason, that reason enables us to perceive. If they did, Hume says, then for saplings to throttle the roots of their parent tree would amount to parricide; we would condemn incest between dogs as well as incest between humans. It is not that an animal does not perceive or employ these moral distinctions because it lacks reason. It is rather that a human makes moral distinctions, has certain feelings, because he or she is human, because of 'the particular constitution of our species'.

Hume compares moral values to secondary qualities. Vice and virtue, he says, are like sounds, colours, heat and cold in being 'not qualities in objects, but perceptions in the mind'. As with secondary qualities, moral values do not exist in nature in the way they are perceived by us. But, just as light waves interact with the rods, cones and retina in your eyes to make you see red, and just as what is red for each of us is red for all, so, according to Hume, each and all of us see murder as abhorrent. Moral, like aesthetic, taste 'has a productive faculty, and gilding or staining all natural objects with the colours, borrowed from internal sentiment, raises in a manner a new creation'. 'Like the perception of beauty and deformity', moral distinctions are 'founded on the original constitution of the human mind, . . . antecedent to all precept or education'.

But – moral disagreement
Although compelling (it has been elaborated into the theory(ies) of moral 'Quasi-realism') Hume's secondary-quality analogy has problems. It doesn't quite jib with the 'look into your own breast, and this is the only fact' theory – for surely you could perceive moral values yet not

act on them. In any case, the analogy is inexact. Despite some cultural differences in colour demarcations, whether an object is red *can* count as true or false (may make a difference in a court-case, for instance); light waves can be objectively analysed, colour blindness detected and discounted for. And indeed Hume is relying on the uniformity of moral perceptions as of secondary qualities, which are presumed to be perceived in a homogeneous, human-specific way (without subjective disparities).

But humans don't, across time and space, share moral taste, or moral perceptions, and they don't have feelings of approval/disapproval regarding the same actions or attributes. It is true that particular actions and attributes are often conceptualized negatively from culture to culture ('murder', 'cruel'), but what is sometimes designated 'murder' can be characterized so as to make it neutral, even praiseworthy ('capital punishment', 'an action in a just war'), depending on the speaker's provisional concerns. The same actions can be differently identified, the same attributes differently applied – what counts as cruel or unjust is open to debate even within the same society, let alone in different ones.

Moral communality via happiness

Such criticisms would not have been as pertinent in Hume's day, when morality was more consensual; and he had the Enlightenment sense of human communality. In any case, he manages to provide a moral criterion that can cut through cultural and personal subjectivities. He does in fact attempt to dig beneath the institution and practices of morality to find more than merely social and cultural objectivity. For he asks a question that is intended to scupper the Moral Rationalist (as it should the Moral Relativist): what do humans want? If there is agreement on that, maybe we can see what morality should be based on; then, all that will be required is empirical research about how it can be achieved.

To be happy, and not to suffer, are the bedrock desires, says Hume – 'the chief spring or actuating principle of the human mind'. He thus provides not only a psychological base for morality but a touchstone for moral decision, and for what is to count as moral. This might sound obvious now that we have been so imbued with late 18th-century Utilitarianism (which was of course inspired by this aspect of Hume's moral philosophy). But we shouldn't underestimate how timely

*Even killing has been considered to be a praiseworthy action in the right context –
many societies, for instance, have promoted capital punishment for criminals.*

'The ultimate ends of human actions can never . . . be accounted for by *reason,* but recommend themselves entirely to the sentiments and affections of mankind . . . Ask a man *why he uses exercise;* he will answer, *because he desires to keep his health.* If you then enquire, *why he desires health,* he will readily reply, *because sickness is painful.* If you push your enquiries farther, and desire a reason *why he hates pain,* it is impossible he can ever give any. This is an ultimate end, and is never referred to any other object.'

David Hume, *An Enquiry concerning the Principles of Human Morals*

Utilitarianism was (and Hume, as pioneer, still more so) in readjusting moral priorities; in reinstating human well-being, rather than religious rules and rigmaroles, at the heart of morality. Admittedly 'well-being' is a question-begging term, and embraces infinitely more than pleasure; but it provides a strong criterion in determining moral issues. Surely Hume is right – to discover true happiness and promote it is what morality, and religion, are actually about.

When judging with 'natural, unprejudiced reason, without the delusive glosses of superstition and false religion', he says, we deem as virtues qualities that are 'useful or agreeable', and that have 'utility' because 'promoting . . . peace, harmony, and order in society', and we dismiss the 'monkish virtues' (celibacy, mortification, self-denial, humility) and their 'gloomy, hair-brained' practitioners. This view, fairly standard in our secular age, was startling in his, and in any case Hume's proto-Utilitarianism is only part of his multi-layered moral philosophy. Unlike Bentham, he has a subtle account of human desires, emotions and motivations, and of how they inform moral behaviour.

But why other people's happiness?
Hume and Utilitarianism say that it is an empirical fact that we all fundamentally desire happiness (and that is probably right). But it is not a fact that we all desire the greatest happiness of the greatest number.

What is supposed to shift the happiness-desiring human from concern for his/her happiness to concern for other people's? Bentham and Mill never satisfactorily bridged this is/ought gap. Hume purports to do so by appealing to 'a [unanimous] natural sentiment of approbation and blame'. We find actions of benevolence, generosity and love 'pleasing', he says, not only when they affect us but in themselves; which shows that our moral sense transcends self-interest. Virtues, because they have 'a natural beauty and amiableness', 'engage our approbation' whether they

Jeremy Bentham was a leading proponent of utilitarianism, but Hume's variant included a subtler account of human desires and motivations.

occur in our immediate vicinity or in far-removed times and places, whenever we hear or read about them, or see them enacted in the theatre. If even animals, which are incapable of artifice, can be kind and altruistic, surely the potential for altruism must be innate and genuine. All of which, Hume declares, surely contradicts Hobbes's 'selfish hypothesis' that we are only capable of self-concern.

But isn't there a very good reason why today we use 'rational' precisely to mean self-interested' as opposed to 'benevolent'? (Hume would be amused at this, and probably use it to tease the Moral Rationalists.) As Erasmus pointed out in *Praise of Folly*, it *is* irrational to Christianly sacrifice my pleasure for somebody else's sake. So why should, and how can, kindness and generosity ever be sufficiently attractive to persuade me to do so? Why should my pleasure in virtue be sufficient to override my desire for pleasure itself and why should my feelings of moral approval have more importance for me than feelings of enjoyment? Isn't Hume too optimistic – in fact unjustified – in assuming that either reason or

Erasmus pointed out that it is irrational to sacrifice one's own pleasure for the sake of another, so how do we ever persuade people to do so?

emotion prompt us to forgo self-interest?

Sympathy

Hume happily acknowledges the problem: there is no *reason* for me not to scratch an itch even if to do so would bring about the destruction of the world; and, conversely, there is no *reason* for me not to cater to the least whim of an Indian at the cost of my total ruin (Hume often refers to India and China as exemplifying countries too far away for him ever to reach).

Hume's rhetoric is hyperbolic; and 'reason' here is very far from the smooth and easy survival instinct he sometimes deems it, but in his moral philosophy he is adamant that reason is 'impotent', except to show us the most effective means of achieving our desires; which, he says, are, by nature, healthily irrational. For there is something in our emotional repertoire which, he says, can explain how we can (without logic) move from is to ought: 'sympathy'.

You may think that he is begging the question by enlisting sympathy – relying on a moral quality when he precisely needs to explain how moral qualities are possible, and thus imperceptibly slipping from is to ought in the very way he condemns. But he is not saying (as some Sentimentalists did) that humans are naturally good. Hume's 'sympathy' does not mean 'compassion', but is a typically Humean mental mechanism that makes compassion possible. It is 'nothing but the conversion of an idea into an impression by the force of the imagination'. Like musical instruments with tautened strings, we are primed to vibrate to other people's emotions. My impression of someone crying automatically transfers my thought to the causes of her grief, which I then, in a sort of emotional contagion, vicariously feel.

Thus 'no man is absolutely indifferent to the happiness and misery of others'. Observing other people's expressions 'excites in our breast a sympathetic movement of pleasure or uneasiness'. We 'suffer for' the stutterer, and, thanks to 'a delicate sympathy for the possessor', enjoy seeing the 'easy and unconstrained' postures of the healthy and vigorous. However selfish, we would never dream of avoiding uncomfortable cobblestones by treading on someone's gouty toes – unless of course he is an enemy.

Sympathy, then, is not virtuous in itself, merely conducive to virtue; 'the chief source of moral distinctions'. It is the mechanism that can elevate us from is to ought, from observation to action, which reason cannot do. Ideally it 'takes us so far out of ourselves, as to give us the same pleasure or uneasiness in the characters of others, as if they had a tendency to our own advantage or loss'. Reason has no influence on the actions and affections, it is 'inert'; has to be activated by desire. Thus 'morality is more properly felt than judg'd of'. Or rather, our judging is, with any luck, appropriately infused with feeling.

Like violins with tautened strings, we are primed to vibrate to the emotions of other people.

Hume opposes not only some of his immediate contemporaries for whom morality was a purely rational matter, but also Plato's view that you just need to understand what is right, for 'no one willingly does wrong'. It is hard to disagree with Hume that ''Tis one thing to know virtue, and another to conform the will to it.' More questionable is his famous utterance: 'Reason is, and ought only to be the slave of the passions, and can never pretend to any other office than to serve and obey them.'

HUME AND NEUROSCIENCE

Neuroscientists have found a neural correlation (which they call 'mirror' neurons) to Hume's notion of metaphorical string-plucking: when experimental subjects view videos of people suffering, the areas of their brains that light up are the same as would light up if they suffered themselves. But scientific confirmation is superfluous. Hume is surely right that, although concern for our own happiness is paramount, we prefer, all things being equal, that others should be happy too.

MORAL IMPARTIALITY – REASON AND THE 'JUDICIOUS OBSERVER'

It is on the basis of Hume's 'sympathy' and 'feelings' texts that Emotivists and Subjectivists enlist him as one of their own. But in fact he is far too sensible and subtle to think that moral statements are just expressions or avowals of emotion. If they were, what could explain the weightiness they purport to bear not just for the person making them but for everyone? How could they (as they do) appeal beyond immediate fellow-feeling, and convey an objective and adjuratory demand? Emotivism and Prescriptivism only account for the emotion involved in moral utterance, and the way it attempts to impose the utterer's taste on other people, but not for why they and their hearers think they are (potentially) justified in this imposition. Hume makes an important distinction:

'When a man denominates another his *enemy*, his *rival*, his *antagonist*, his *adversary*, he is understood to speak the language of self-love, and to express sentiments, peculiar to himself, and arising from his particular circumstances and situation. But when he bestows on any man the epithets of *vicious* or *odious* or *depraved*, he then speaks another language, and expresses sentiments, in which he expects all his audience are to concur with him. He must here, therefore, depart from his private and particular situation, and must choose a point of view, common to him with others; he must move some universal principle of the human frame, and touch a string to which all mankind have an accord and symphony.'

PASSIONS

The word 'passions' in 18th-century parlance refers to emotions generally, and not (as now) to dramatic feelings; indeed, Hume declares that the 'calm', as opposed to the 'violent', passions are often so serene as to mistaken for reasonings.

He realizes that sympathy's strings are not attuned to the universal symphony, because our feelings are localized. Our sympathy is often weaker than our self-concern, and fainter for strangers and people remote from us than for family and friends. It can simply amount to distracting sentimentality: Hitler wept at Lehar's music; Himmler banned hunting.

'The public good is indifferent to us, except so far as sympathy interests us in it', which it doesn't automatically do. Hume enlists reason so as to account for morality's wide-ranging impartiality. Reason, he says, can extend our 'limited generosity' and limited imagination by putting what looms large in our vicinity into proportion with what only *seems* small because distant to us. Thus, by 'correcting the appearance by reflexion', we balance out self-interest and bias, and 'form some general inalterable

Our sympathy is often most attuned to those closest to us – even Hitler loved dogs.

standard' by which to judge moral worth, correcting the heart's view with the 'universal abstract' one. And, adding to the clutter in his moral armoury, Hume borrows Adam Smith's 'impartial spectator' when saying that we often do, and ought to, bring our feelings into line with what a 'judicious observer' would judge appropriate. Optimistically, Hume declares that 'reason and sentiment concur in almost all moral determinations and conclusions'.

Hume borrowed Adam Smith's idea of the 'impartial spectator' to work out what we should and shouldn't do.

Artificial virtues

He also distinguishes 'natural virtues' and 'selfish virtues' (which are easy on the emotions) from 'artificial virtues'. These 'produce pleasure and approbation by means of an artifice or contrivance, which arises from the circumstances and necessities of mankind' – an artifice superadded by society to the natural internal mechanism of sympathy. Justice, for instance, which would be unnecessary in any society that could provide sufficient for all its citizens, is, in all known societies, publicly useful. The motive to it is too 'sublime' to affect most people, and we don't approve each instance of it – far from it: an individual act of justice may conflict with our own self-interest or our children's, or may seem unduly stern. But we approve of justice as a whole system, overall. Once a system of justice is in place, the 'sense of honour and duty' in obeying its rules 'follows *naturally* and of itself', though it is also 'augmented' by the further artifice of penalties, punishments and attention to children's upbringing. 'Tho' justice be artificial, the sense of its morality is [or becomes] natural'.

Hume includes promise-keeping among the artificial virtues. He calls it 'one of the most mysterious and incomprehensible operations' imaginable, for it 'changes entirely the nature of an external object, and even of a human creature', rather (he jokingly says) like transubstantiation. In promising, we don't describe (our feelings) but create (a commitment). The very words have an effect on our will and conjure up an obligation.

Thus the artificial virtues 'give a new direction to [the] natural passions, and teach us that we can better satisfy our appetites in an oblique and artificial manner, than by their headlong and impetuous motion'.

OBJECTIONS (ADDED TO THOSE MADE EN PASSANT)

1) Can all these variegated moral accounts combine? How effective are they even separately? Doesn't he himself fudge is and ought?

2) Sometimes he is descriptive where he might be more penetratingly sceptical. He assumes that our prepossessions in favour of certain qualities are innate. He often talks as if he thinks that all humans are alike across time and space ('Would you know the sentiments, inclinations, and course of life of the Greeks and Romans? Study well the temper and actions of the French and English'), and (almost as his rationalist opponents do) that morality is perennial and universal. He does, however, make some allowance for the shifts of moral argument, and admits that what counts as virtuous can change – courage was estimated highly by the Romans, now (due to Christianity) benevolence has superseded it.

3) If what counts as virtuous is what pleases us, how does he distinguish pleasing but neutral qualities, such as wit, beauty and wealth, from virtues? In some ways he would prefer not to. He objects to the way religion has put morals 'on a like footing with civil laws' so that 'we' (18th-century people), unlike 'the ancients', praise deliberately exercised constraints at the expense of 'pleasing', effortless endowments. He says he will avoid the terms 'vice' and 'virtue' (though doesn't), and account wit and beauty as good, and barrenness and misfortune as virtually vice.

4) But in so far as he holds 'personal merit' to consist 'entirely in the usefulness or agreeableness of qualities to the person himself possessed of them, or to others who have any intercourse with him' he is perhaps too aesthetic and heartless. Certainly he runs foul of our contemporary

morality, and of his own compelling notion of 'sympathy' and his eagerness to move us (and explain how we move) from self-interested to impartial approbation. In exalting the vigorous ancient Greek morality so beloved of Nietzsche, however, he is rectifying what is joyless and petty in the Christian morality of his time.

5) Although he says that the agent's motives are what we praise and blame, he seems more concerned with actions and the results of actions. But this is not just due to his aesthetic morality. As with today's Virtue Ethics, he emphasizes the character as a whole, moral training, and the 'durable principles of the mind'.

6) Neither Hume's mechanistic way of explaining our moral motivations, nor his assertion that experience shows us to have it, is wholly satisfactory: what are the causes of us having such (limited) sympathy as we do possess?

He relies on feeling, which may not be forthcoming. We 'unavoidably feel . . .' he continually says – but do we? – and only 'the depraved', like Nero, or those with 'a cold insensibility, or narrow selfishness of temper' don't possess 'sympathy'. But how many are depraved and insensible? He says that Nero was warped by flattery and his unnatural status, but by the same token all of us are influenced by our upbringings. Sympathy and ensuing virtue may be less part of our human make-up, more the result of social factors, than Hume thinks. His moral philosophy is addressed to people of the right sort, nice civilized people like him, with well-functioning mirror neurons. But what about the others?

7) Even if Hume's account of morality works in a broad-based way as an explanation of how morality is set up and flourishes, it does not account for the variations of moral code across cultures and individuals. In fact, it relies on a certain synchronicity of sentiment without which morality would degenerate into arbitrariness and subjectivity – and that degeneration has to some extent been Hume's legacy.

Key points

- Hume points to a devastating problem for moral thinkers: they write as if what we ought to do can be inferred from the way the world is, but it can't be.

- In answer to the question of what prompts us to enact moral values, he suggests that by nature we have a moral sense, that we perceive and feel what is good or bad.

- Hume says a desire for happiness and aversion from pain provides universal motivation.

- As a way of explaining how we move from desire for personal happiness to desire for general happiness, he says we have 'sympathy' – a natural proclivity to prefer, all things being equal, that those around us are happy and at ease rather than distressed.

- Hume also asks us to imagine a 'judicious observer' of our actions.

- Reason, he says, helps to transform natural into artificial virtues, such as justice.

- Hume intertwines the personal and emotional with the reasoned, universal aspects of morality.

Chapter 8

Jean-Jacques Rousseau (1712–78)

Vagabond and maverick, Rousseau was a figure of the Counter-Enlightenment who toppled Enlightenment into Romanticism. He never actually used the term 'noble savage' that is so often attributed to him, but he fomented the cult of primitivism and a corresponding suspicion of civilization and the intellect. 'I venture to declare that a state of reflection is a state contrary to nature, and that a thinking man is a depraved animal,' he wrote. He seems to have had a premonition that nature would soon be tamed and despoiled.

Wilderness was not loved while it was threatening, and for centuries humankind had shut it out and tried to subdue it. Even in the 17th century, travellers in carriages crossing Derbyshire would pull down the blinds to avoid seeing 'Nature's pudenda' – the 'deformed' crags and rocks. But in the early 19th century the blinds went rattling up. The Industrial Revolution had begun during the Enlightenment, and what with Kant's 'sublime' (see p.180) and Rousseau's 'solitary walker', nature was now craved and revered, and the Romantics rushed to as wild a countryside as still remained.

NATURE HAS MADE MAN HAPPY AND GOOD

Rousseau is sometimes coupled with Freud, but while Freud detected terrifying subterranean impulses for which civilization is the necessary, if regrettable, curb, Rousseau declared the state of nature, both in human history and in childhood, to be innocent, docile and almost emotion-free. He was adamant that 'Nature has made man happy and good, and society deprives him and makes him miserable', although his writings vary as to how inevitable and unfortunate the emergence of society is.

Rousseau was an outsider and a figure of the Counter-Enlightenment, which marked the beginning of the Romantic movement.

As well as philosophy, Rousseau wrote on politics, anthropology, education, music, economics and botany. He influenced philosophers as diverse as Kant and Marx, and inspired educational theory and a range of political views – socialism, liberalism, totalitarianism, nationalism. Polish nationalists and Corsican rebels asked him to write the new constitutions for their prospective independent states. The French revolutionaries would claim him as their own. His political philosophy is hard to interpret and would be harder to implement, the idea of 'the general will' being particularly unfathomable.

Although excoriating the arts for corrupting public morals, he wrote plays and the century's best-selling novel, *Julie, or The New Heloise*, and composed a ballet and operas (his operetta 'The Village Soothsayer', much loved by Madame de Pompadour, was performed at the wedding of the future Louis XVI and Marie Antoinette). Rousseau's autobiography, *The Confessions* (published posthumously), was 'an undertaking hitherto without precedent' to present 'the likeness of a

Rousseau grew up in the Calvinist city of Geneva, where he learned much from the classics, despite having no formal education.

ROUSSEAU THE SERVANT

One of the whimsical and inexplicable acts for which Rousseau always reproached himself was when, as a servant in a grand household, he stole a valuable piece of ribbon and, when the theft was discovered, accused the pretty cook (whom he found very attractive). She was consequently dismissed.

man in all the truth of nature'. It established a new and lasting trend for frank revelation.

Jean-Jacques Rousseau was born on 28 June 1712 in the Calvinist city of Geneva, son to a watch-maker. His mother, who came from a cultured family, left a good library when she died a few days after his birth, and from reading aloud to his father as he worked, Rousseau developed 'a sound taste', despite having no formal education. Plutarch's *Lives of Noble Greeks and Romans* inspired his love of Sparta and republicanism. When his father fled Geneva to avoid arrest, Rousseau, aged ten, was boarded out for two years with a village pastor and his sister. Her occasional chastisements led him to develop, or recognize, a taste (as yet unnamed) for being spanked, as he discusses in the *Confessions*.

Aged 16 and apprenticed to a Genevan engraver, Rousseau returned late from a country walk, and finding the city gates locked, ran away. He spent his youth wandering around Switzerland and France, snatching occasional work (as servant, secretary, tutor, music teacher and music copyist), and both courting and resenting benefactors. Not only did he clash with Enlightenment urbanity but with virtually every friend he ever made.

His first, and intermittent, patron was Madame de Warens, who oversaw his conversion to Catholicism (he even began training to be a priest), and encouraged his reading. Twelve years older than he was, she was Maman, and he her 'little one' –even after he became her lover. In 1740, he met Condillac and D'Alembert, major Enlightenment figures, and, later, Diderot, with whom he became fierce friends until the inevitable falling-out, and for whose *Encyclopedia* he wrote several entries on music. In 1749, Diderot was imprisoned in Vincennes for his unorthodox views, and, walking to visit him, Rousseau saw an advertisement for an essay competition on whether moral improvement had been advanced by the revival of the arts and sciences. Instantly inspired, he 'became an author almost in spite of [him]self'. He won the competition with his *Discourse on the Arts and Sciences,* and immediate celebrity. A series of tolerant aristocrats offered him a series of beautiful lodgings in which, for the next 12 years, he wrote prolifically and produced his best work. All his misfortunes stemmed from that 'moment of madness' on the Vincennes road, he later bitterly wrote.

Baronness de Warens was Rousseau's first patron and had a great influence on Rousseau's life.

In 1745 Rousseau had met Thérèse Levasseur, a barely literate chambermaid, who was his mistress, and eventually his wife, until he died. Visitors often took her for the housekeeper, and Rousseau, for all his rage at inequality, seems to have treated her as such and to have felt free to form romantic attachments to high-born ladies, including Sophie d'Houdetot, apparently the only woman with whom he ever fell in love. Each time Therese had a child (five in all), Rousseau would immediately place it in the foundling home, as, to his fury, Voltaire revealed in an anonymous pamphlet.

In 1754, Rousseau reconverted to Calvinism and resumed Genevan citizenship, but he lost his much-proclaimed love for his birthplace when *The Social Contract* and *Emile* (both published in 1762) were banned and burned there, as well as in Paris, and a warrant was issued for his arrest. He fled Geneva, and later Motiers in France when his house was stoned. Hume offered him refuge in England, but soon Rousseau

Rousseau is credited with creating the idea of the 'noble savage', which has been used to critique present day European society.

was convinced that Hume was part of the plot against him which he suspected everywhere. Increasingly alienated from his former friends and the Enlightenment mainstream, perpetually on the move to avoid prosecution, he eventually died of apoplexy in 1778, and was buried on an island in a friend's garden. In 1794, during the Terror after the French Revolution, a triumphant procession of revolutionaries, carrying copies of *The Social Contract*, moved his body to the Panthéon in Paris.

Discourse on the Arts and Sciences

When Rousseau saw the advertisement for the Dijon essay competition he was suddenly dazzled and giddy, flooded with ideas. He later said that if he could only have written a fraction of what he then saw and felt as he lay trembling under an oak tree, he would have exposed all the contradictions and abuses of social institutions and demonstrated how man is naturally good, and has only become bad because of these institutions. All his future writing, however inconsistent, was informed by that vision.

'Whether the restoration of the sciences and the arts has contributed to purifying morals' was the question proposed by the Dijon Academy. Rousseau's answer at first seems to celebrate European Enlightenment. It had, he says, come from 'the least expected quarter: the stupid Muslim, eternal scourge of letters', who had, by conquering Constantinople, effected the rediscovery of Plato and Aristotle, and other 'debris' from ancient Greece. But then Rousseau parts company with his Enlightenment friends. The revival of the arts and sciences, he says, serves to 'spread garlands of flowers over the iron chains with which men are burdened', stifle men's innate sense of freedom and make them love their slavery. The 'much vaunted urbanity' that Enlightenment has brought corrupts 'natural and rustic' morals. Because it teaches our emotions to speak 'in ready-made terms', it makes people competitive, insincere, treacherous. The arts are generated from idleness, and in turn generate it, promoting time-wasting, excessive luxury and vice, dissipating vigour, military virtues and love of Fatherland. This is what ruined Egypt, Greece, Rome, Constantinople, and China, and will ruin us. 'The savages of America who go around totally naked and live only off the products of their hunting' have, in contrast, 'proved impossible to tame'.

Present-day readers of the first *Discourse* may be baffled by its hotchpotch of left-wing and right-wing positions, its mixture of what would now be described as politically correct and incorrect views. They should remember that Rousseau, who managed to be liberal, socialist and reactionary, was largely responsible for such categories being invented at all.

Discourse on Inequality

'What is the origin of inequality among men, and whether it is authorized by natural law' was the essay competition question for what became Rousseau's second *Discourse* – it didn't win. He diagnoses two types of inequality – natural or physical, and moral or political; and, in order to explain the source of the second type, envisages what pre-social humanity would (or might) have been like. 'Savage man', he says, was 'limited at first to mere sensations' and 'destitute of every species of intelligence'. 'The only goods he recognizes in the universe are food, a female, and sleep: the only evils he fears are hunger and pain.' Because he had so few, and such 'inactive', emotions other than 'pitié' (an instinct similar to Hume's sympathy), and had no moral obligations, he was 'an

LOVING THE SELF

Amour de soi (love of self) is the natural, instinctual love of self which, in humans and animals, ensures attention to biological needs and self-preservation;

amour-propre (self-love) is the social, artificial love of self which depends on, and craves, other people's esteem, and is competitive.

equal stranger to war and to all ties . . . and would have spent his days insensibly in peace and innocence'.

Rousseau is proto-Darwinian: he envisages the primitive human as virtually one of the animals, weaker and less agile than some, but better organized. Yet he is un-Darwinian in insisting that 'natural men' were not herd creatures. Humans (he says) did not live in groups but wandered solitary and pacific in the forest, rarely sleeping in the same place for more than one night, and having wordless sex after which 'they parted with the same indifference'. For happily polygamous natural man, 'every woman equally answers his purpose'. Women suckled their children, who, as soon as they were strong enough to forage for themselves, would leave their mothers and quickly become incapable of recognizing one another if they happened to meet again.

Neither goodness nor badness was possible in this forest Eden. Humanity's undoing began when humans started to abandon 'their original wildness', ceasing to be wholly creatures of sensation, and developing 'a kind of reflection'.

Locke had argued that there was property-ownership before civil society began; but Rousseau's equivalent of the Fall (the eating of the forbidden fruit) was not when humans were exiled from a garden but when 'someone first enclosed a plot of ground', and then persuaded the others that it was his. From how many crimes, wars, murders, horrors and misfortunes could mankind have been saved, exclaims Rousseau, if only someone had pulled up the stakes or filled the ditch, and 'cried to his fellows "Beware of listening to this impostor; you are undone if you once forget that the fruits of the earth belong to us all, and the earth itself to nobody."'

'Nothing is more gentle than man in his primitive state, as he is placed by nature at an equal distance from the stupidity of brutes, and the fatal ingenuity of civilized man.'

Rousseau, *Discourse on Inequality*

Once there was property, humans formed into families and groups. They developed agriculture and metallurgy, which gave them leisure for dancing and singing, during which they competed over who was the most handsome, strong, dexterous or elegant. Distinction-making and evaluation were 'the first steps towards inequality'. Self-preserving *amour de soi* became self-regarding *amour-propre*. The desire for esteem, to which they all claimed a right, bred self-consciousness, affectation, deceit, competition, emotionality and artificial needs. The social contract was a con-trick perpetrated by the wily and powerful on the simple who 'all ran headlong into their chains'.

The second *Discourse* was nicknamed 'Essay against Civilization'. Rousseau begins and ends it on a note of regret – that the natural human has been distorted, like the statue of Glaucus which was so disfigured by time, seas and tempests that it now looks more like a beast than a god. But he agrees that it is difficult to distinguish properly between what is original and what is artificial, or to tell how much is the effect of the divine will as opposed to human art.

Most scholars insist that Rousseau was not advocating a return to the wild, but the Appendix to the second *Discourse* exhorts the reader to 'retire to the woods' and 'renounce the enlightenment of your species in order to renounce its vices'.

The Social Contract

Chapter One famously opens: 'Man is born free, and everywhere he is in chains.' But there is already ambiguity. '*Est né*' could mean 'is born' or 'was born'. Rousseau could be saying that (as with Original Sin) humankind was born free but is now fettered, or that enslavement happens anew after each person's birth. Either way, he goes on to ask how freedom was (or is)

On receiving the *Discourse on Inequality*, Voltaire wrote: 'I have received your new book against the human race, and thank you for it. Never was such a cleverness used in the design of making us all stupid. One longs, in reading your book, to walk on all fours. But as I have lost that habit for more than sixty years, I feel unhappily the impossibility of resuming it. Nor can I embark in search of the savages of Canada, because the maladies to which I am condemned render a European surgeon necessary to me; because war is going on in those regions; and because the example of our actions has made the savages nearly as bad as ourselves.'

Voltaire, *Letter to Rousseau*, 1762

lost, which he says he doesn't know, and what can make it legitimate – a question he thinks he can answer.

Unlike in the second *Discourse*, where he seemed to hanker for the state of nature and considered the social contract fraudulent, here Rousseau says that humans must have reached a stage in their history where the obstacles to preservation proved greater than each individual's strength to outweigh them. Unless they had formed a social pact, humans would have died out. He tries to work out the best and most justifiable form of social bondage in which 'each man recovers the equivalent of everything he loses, and in the bargain acquires more power to preserve what he has', so that, 'while uniting himself with all, he still obeys himself alone, and remains as free as before'.

More than Locke, if less than Hobbes, Rousseau wants the 'union of public persons' created by the social contract to be strongly cohesive. But whereas for Hobbes, cohesion is achieved because the sovereign, as a formidable power, bestrides the disparate individuals, for Rousseau, the sovereign *is* the people 'when it plays an active role' (in its passive role, it is 'the state'; it 'can act only when the people is assembled'). Each individual, who in himself is entirely complete and solitary, is transformed into 'part of a much greater whole' – a single body with a collective will. This 'general will' is not the sum of individual desires, perhaps arbitrated by means of voting. It is what, jointly, we all 'really' want, even though 'we do not always discern what that is'. Laws are 'nothing other than authentic acts of the general will', which is directed towards 'the common preservation and general well-being', and which is 'always unchanging, incorruptible and pure'.

There is voting in Rousseau's state, but each individual is expected to vote not on the basis of whether they approve or disapprove of the motion, but of whether or not it is in accordance with the general will. If 'an opinion contrary to my own prevails, this proves only that I have made a mistake, and that what I believed to be the general will was not so'.

That this sounds ominously totalitarian is partly due to history – the general will would become a catchphrase of the French Revolution, and Robespierre, while ordering executions, would quote passages from *The Social Contract* – yet, whatever its undertones, Rousseau is right that in any state, however liberal, the citizen has to obey the laws, whether they like them or not. Nonetheless, in a liberal state, a citizen can contest the laws, whereas Rousseau pronounces that, if necessary, the dissident 'shall be forced to be free'. Others know better than you what freedom is (and probably what happiness should rightly be as well). Somehow, and rather inexplicably, 'The sovereign by the mere fact that it is, is always all that it ought to be.'

There is no one form of government that is best for all states, according to Rousseau, but, if ruled by law, any state counts as a republic. He doubts that there has ever been a democracy, and deems it conducive to civil war, although possibly workable in a very small state. Monarchy sometimes 'suits' large states, but it is open to arbitrary favouritism and abuse of power. Government by aristocrats is 'the best and most

KANT AND ROUSSEAU

It may seem odd that Immanuel Kant, one of the originators of the idea of human rights, should be an ardent admirer of Rousseau. His categorical imperative would subtly reiterate Rousseau's paradox that true freedom consists in obeying the laws that you yourself ordain.

Despite his liberal views, Rousseau had little respect for democracy, which he thought could only work in very small states.

natural arrangement for the wisest to govern the multitude', provided they govern for its advantage, not their own. He advocates small states, united by common aims and a nationalist sentiment, which goes against the universalism of some Enlightenment thinkers, and he would almost certainly oppose globalism and multi-culturalism.

Again, laws can vary depending on the sort of state they bind, but Rousseau favours exile or capital punishment for those who question or countermand the general will, whatever it turns out to be. To do so is to forfeit your membership of the state. You will be killed 'less as a citizen than as an enemy'.

Privately, citizens can believe the variegations of any creed they please, but they must hold and publicly profess the 'simple and few' dogmas of the newly created civil religion. These will forbid intolerance (except towards atheists, who cannot be trusted), and affirm the existence of God

and an afterlife, the happiness of the just, the punishment of sinners, and the sanctity of the social contract and state. Thereby divine worship could be harnessed to a love of the laws, and the homeland would be made an object of adoration. Man, thanks to Rousseau's social contract, would (says Rousseau) lose his 'natural liberty' but gain 'moral freedom'. In the 20th century, Bertrand Russell wrote, 'Hitler is an outcome of Rousseau; Roosevelt and Churchill, of Locke.'

PROPERTY AND LIBERTY

Rousseau's second *Discourse* is the original source of hatred for property. In *The Social Contract,* however, he approves property-owning, as long as it is based on a legal title, and not on force or 'the right of the first occupant'. The legal right to property is, it turns out, what man gains by the social contract, along with civil liberty.

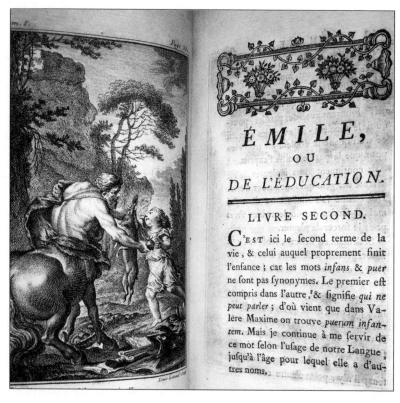

In Emile, *Rousseau laid out his approach to education.*

EMILE, OR ON EDUCATION

'Everything is good as it leaves the hands of the Author of things; everything degenerates in the hands of man.' The first sentence of the first chapter of *Emile*, might, for someone who has read no other Rousseau, seem to follow the Christian tradition of the Fall in which divine goodness was traduced by human sinfulness. But Rousseau believes precisely the opposite. Rather than the baby being born in original sin, 'there is no original perversity in the human heart'. Not a single vice in the grown adult, he says, cannot be traced back to when it was implanted in the originally innocent child. Enlightenment notions of happiness and progress entailed theorizing about children's upbringing and education, but even Locke, despite his unusually liberal ideas on the subject, considered no child to be

Rousseau, an admirer of the Spartans, argued that an important part of a child's education was learning how to bear pain and fatigue.

sufficiently tabula rasa as not to require a drilling in virtue that went against the grain. Rousseau, who declared childhood to be 'unknown', almost single-handedly invented it and originated the notion of childish innocence.

Rousseau's education system sounds tough, however. An admirer of the Spartans, he strongly advised against mollycoddling. 'Nature hardens' and children can learn to bear pain and fatigue. Although claiming it 'an incontestable maxim that the first movements of nature are always right', it often sounds as if the representative child, in this mixture of narrative and exhortation, is to be very early inducted into Rousseau's

> ## SOPHIE
>
> Rousseau began a sequel to *Emile (Emile and Sophie)* in which after their initial happiness, Sophie is unfaithful and Emile becomes a slave to an Algerian prince. According to some sources, Rousseau intended them to reunite, possibly with Emile having acquired a second wife; but the novel was never finished.

(questionably) ideal state. Anyone in civil society who wants to preserve the primacy of natural feelings, says Rousseau, 'will be nothing' because 'always floating between his inclinations and his duties'. He 'does not know what he wants' – does not, presumably, have a proper sense of the 'general will'.

Rousseau began writing *Emile* 'to gratify a good mother who knows how to think', and it expanded from a pamphlet to a five-volume novel-cum-education manual. No one, he says loves seeing children 'romp and play' more than he does. Having abandoned all of his own, he feels entitled to prescribe to the 'good mother' that her baby should be breastfed, unswaddled, and sleep in a large cradle, and to appoint himself as the devoted guardian painstakingly teaching Emile, although he always seems to have hated teaching. Many of his educational methods have been adopted. Emile should, and in fact does, learn about mathematical measuring from practical tasks ('Here is quite a large stream. How shall we cross it? Will one of the planks from the courtyard reach both banks?'); but arguably it has proved counterproductive to apply to a whole class of reluctant children what was designed for a single child with an omnipresent teacher.

Inevitably the child in this educational experiment is male, but in the fifth, and last, book, Emile is supplied with a female companion, Sophie. In an early essay, Rousseau speculated that if women had been given more of a say in governing, business and the arts, they might have surpassed men. In the first *Discourse*, he declared that women's natural power over men could, if women were given better education, be better directed. In *Emile*, though, he pronounces the quest for abstract and speculative truths to be beyond woman's competence, and Sophie is virtually uneducated.

'Woman is made specially to please man', therefore 'ought to make herself pleasing to him rather than to provoke him'. It is not enough that she is estimable, she 'must be esteemed'. The very qualities that he lamented humans acquiring when trapped into social life – servility, self-consciousness, admiration-seeking, emotionality – are ones that he considers women to have by nature, and that he exhorts them to foster. For Rousseau, women in fact seem not to be fully human, just an afterthought. Only because 'it is not good for Emile to be alone' is Sophie 'given to' him (echoes of Adam's rib). Like any little girl she will have learned to read and write 'with repugnance' but spent hours dressing and undressing her doll – a 'definite primary taste' that merely requires to be directed towards the sewing skills she will enjoy.

The part of *Emile* that was most responsible for its being banned was the long section 'Profession of Faith by a Savoyard Vicar'. Like Spinoza, the fictitious priest (probably voicing Rousseau's own views) dismisses miracles and religious revelation, and deplores intolerance between different faiths. But he strongly believes in ('or rather, I sense') God, the wise, powerful will that governs the world. Following conscience, the 'voice of the soul' which 'never deceives', he wants to subdue 'the empire of the senses and the passions which are their ministers' and be raised to the love of justice and moral beauty.

Rousseau is often accused of inconsistency in making this standard distinction between base senses and lofty spirit, but in fact a strain of conventional prudishness runs through his work. Certainly in the second *Discourse* he prefers the savage's blithely undiscriminating 'physical love' to the 'moral love' that pins sexual desire to one particular object and is 'the rule and bridle of nature's inclinations'. That is a 'factitious feeling', cunningly fostered by women so as to promote their power over 'the sex they ought to obey', and only developed due to the unnecessary rise of competitive *amour propre*. But he also shows distaste for sexual desire, which he pronounces not to be a 'true need' but only an 'alleged' one, inflamed by 'lewd objects' and 'indecent ideas' without which we might remain effortlessly chaste. It sometimes seems that he bitterly revisits his own seduction by Madame de Warens – probably unconsciously. No more than anyone else, for all his declarations to the contrary, did Rousseau really know 'the feelings of his heart'.

'The limbs of a growing child should be free to move easily in his clothing; nothing should cramp their growth or movement', wrote Rousseau in Emile – an ideal on display in Thomas Gainsborough's The Painter's Daughters Chasing a Butterfly.

Key points

- Rousseau is a turbulent, inconsistent thinker, but he invariably inveighs against corruption, whether by the arts and sciences, property, competitiveness, society, women – or the Enlightenment.

- *Discourse on the Arts and Sciences* recounts, and regrets, how the effeminizing influence of the arts has sapped men's natural vigour.

- *Discourse on Inequality* gives a hypothetical account of how humans lost their original benignly amoral state and became self-aware, property-owning, rivalrous and unequal. 'He who first enclosed a plot of ground', according to Rousseau, was a mixture of Satan and Eve.

- In *The Social Contract*, Rousseau declares society with all its restrictions to be inevitable; but he tries to formulate the best compromise between loss of individual freedom and gain of social liberty. The 'general will' must prevail, although how it is to be discerned remains mysterious.

- In most of his works, Rousseau insists that we are born naturally virtuous: any vice observable in adulthood can only have been implanted by society.

- *Emile* advises on the best way of educating a (male) child. Learning by discovery is recommended.

- In *The Confessions*, in which he sets out to show himself 'vile and despicable, good, high-minded and sublime, according as I was one or the other', Rousseau started the cult of authenticity.

Chapter 9

Immanuel Kant (1724–1804): Epistemology and Metaphysics

Immanuel Kant is widely considered the greatest philosopher since Plato and Aristotle. His philosophy spans and interlinks metaphysics, ethics, aesthetics, anthropology, politics and natural science. It had a huge influence, most immediately on Hegel, Schopenhauer and German Idealism, but also on all subsequent epistemology, metaphysics, ethics (in practice as well as theory) and aesthetics.

Kant's 'Copernican Revolution' rescued metaphysics from the sceptical impasse in which it was stuck. Scientific discovery and the various developments of Descartes' 'mechanical philosophy' all revealed a world which scarcely accommodated the old certainties of free will, the soul and God, or even allowed the possibility of being perceived. Kant turned the problem round, arguing that, for knowledge to be possible, our perceiving and thinking must be structured in advance of experiencing, and he set out to investigate the cognitive structures necessary if we are to know anything at all.

Just as 'the understanding is itself the law-giver of nature', so, according to Kant, we are responsible for making moral laws – laws which are not dependent on our desires but on pure practical reason. The test for whether an action is permissible is whether the agent is prepared for everyone else to do it as well. A supporter of liberty and the French Revolution, Kant emphasized the way we are equal members of a moral community, and that morality is based on impartiality and consistency.

His moral philosophy has also influenced political philosophy. Kant was an essential part of the liberal tradition (before 'liberal' became a dirty word synonymous with capitalist ruthlessness). The American

Kant's philosophy spanned metaphysics, ethics, aesthetics and even politics.

20th-century philosopher John Rawls urged us to adopt a thought experiment similar to Kant's when deciding on the principles of justice in a society: we should imagine choosing them from behind a 'veil of ignorance', which screens what ethnicity, gender, sexuality or class we will have in the society, and whether or not we will be able-bodied, intelligent and attractive.

In Kant's aesthetics, he discusses 'the sublime' – a concept which originated in first-century Rome for what is vast and awe-inspiring in nature, as opposed to the tamer 'beautiful'. Threatening cliffs, thunderclouds, volcanoes, the boundless sea – the terror these would arouse in 'an untutored man' (says Kant) can be transformed into a reminder of our moral freedom. Our 'physical sensibility' is enabled to 'look out beyond itself into the infinite, which for it is an abyss', because realizing that reason, rather than being dwarfed by nature, dominates it both outside and within us. Kant's 'sublime' and his interiorization of nature greatly influenced Romantic poets and artists. 'To me / High mountains are a feeling', wrote Byron.

KANT'S LIFE

Born on 22 April 1724, Kant was the son of a harness-maker in the Prussian town of Königsberg (now Kaliningrad). His family were fervent Pietists (a low-church Protestant sect) and, thanks to an influential pastor, Kant was sent to a strict Pietist school, which he hated (in later life he never attended church). At 16, he entered Königsberg University where he studied classics, physics and philosophy, doing private teaching to support not only himself but also his siblings after his father died

Kant's idea of the sublime found expression in the art of the Romantics, as seen, for example, in Caspar David Friedrich's Wanderer above the Sea of Fog *c. 1814.*

virtually penniless in 1746. He left the university without a degree, aged 24, to become a private family tutor, but returned seven years later and handed in his philosophy dissertation. For the next 15 years he gave public lectures on geography, meteorology, astronomy, physics, anthropology and mathematics, worked as a librarian, wrote treatises on theology and philosophy, and twice applied unsuccessfully for a professorship before at last becoming a salaried professor at the age of 46.

Like mathematicians, most philosophers do their best work when young, but in his 'pre-critical' phase, Kant did nothing of much importance. 'I have the fortune to be a lover of metaphysics, but my mistress has shown me few favours as yet,' he wrote at the age of 42. It was when he was 46 that reading Hume woke him, as he said, from his 'dogmatic slumbers'. He then spent 11 years writing his vast revolutionary *Critique of Pure Reason*, the first edition of which was published in 1781 when he was 57. *Prolegomena to any Future Metaphysics* (a shorter, more accessible version of the *Critique*) appeared two years later, the *Groundwork for the Metaphysics of Morals* in 1785, a second edition of the *Critique* in 1787, the *Critique of Practical Reason* (moral philosophy) in 1788, and, in 1790, the *Critique of Judgment* (aesthetics and teleology).

Religion within the Bounds of Reason Alone (1793) earned him a reprimand from King Frederick William II, to whom Kant wrote to 'declare solemnly' that he would not publicly discourse on religion again, although he felt absolved from his promise when the king died a few years later. He only stopped teaching when he was 74, and produced essays and several more books, including *Metaphysics of Morals* (1797) before the mental decline of his last six years.

Kant never travelled more than a few miles from Königsberg, and, although he taught geography, almost certainly never saw mountains or the sea. Königsbergers set their clocks by him, for at precisely 3.30 each day he would sally forth for his afternoon walk under the linden trees. He was a small man of 1.57m (5ft 2in), with a sunken chest, disproportionately large head, bright blue eyes and lopsided body; a self-confessed hypochondriac who suffered from indigestion, and was fussy about his bowels, 'sensitive nerves' and dress. He sometimes wore gold-bordered coats, and sported a gold-knobbed stick or a ceremonial sword. His silk stockings were held up by bands which ran up under his trousers

Kant was publicly reprimanded by the Prussian King Frederick William II for his controversial statements about religion.

> 'All the interests of my reason, speculative as well as practical, combine in the three following questions:
>
> 1 What can I know?
>
> 2 What ought I to do?
>
> 3 What may I hope?'
>
> Immanuel Kant, *Critique of Pure Reason*

into his pockets, where each of them ended in springs contained in a tiny box (his own invention).

Twice he contemplated marrying, but in both cases was so indecisive that the prospective wife gave up. Sexual love, which he probably never experienced, he considered to be mere appetite, after satisfying which its object 'is cast aside as one casts a lemon which has been sucked dry'. He disliked music, apart from military marches, judging it the lowest of the arts 'because it merely plays with sensations'.

Kant called his metaphysical writings 'dry, obscure, contrary to all ordinary ideas, and on top of that prolix', and he deprecated the monotonous 'hammering' of his 'repetitious' lectures; yet, according to his pupils, he was 'full of playfulness, wit and humour', always seemed to be thinking through problems afresh as he talked, and could move his listeners to tears. To be sure of a place at his lectures, students had to arrive an hour early, at six in the morning. He was much in demand at grand Königsberg dinner parties for his witty, erudite conversation, but could be dismayingly forthright. He defended the philosopher Moses Mendelssohn so vigorously as to be thought rude, and enthused about the French Revolution. He squared that enthusiasm with his disapproval of rebellion by declaring that since the king had abdicated, the Estates General now represented France. Eagerness to hear news of the storming of the Bastille made him actually miss his afternoon walk; the only other time he missed it was because he was so absorbed in *Emile*, Rousseau's subversive tract on education.

Moses Mendelssohn, a figure of the Jewish Enlightenment, was vigorously defended by Kant.

Kant believed that 'to compose character is our duty'. Although his own self-creation was not the florid Romantic sort, and his deep admiration for the wild Rousseau might seem incongruous, the two men were similar in their dogged pursuit of authenticity. Far from being at odds with his love of freedom, Kant's uncompromisingly eccentric self-discipline was an expression of it.

METAPHYSICS

There was no metaphysical problem that Kant hadn't solved, or at least provided the key to solving – or so he himself proclaims in the preface to the *Critique of Pure Reason*. He can imagine the reader's expression of indignation and contempt at such arrogance, he says, but how much more arrogant are the 'dogmatic philosophers' who claim to prove the simple nature of the soul or the necessity of the world's beginning without an 'antecedent critique' of the powers of reason. He compares these extreme rationalists to the dove that, thinking her wings are impeded by the air's resistance, tries to fly beyond the earth's atmosphere – but finds nothing to sustain her flight. They end up only analysing concepts we already have, or using concepts that have nothing to correspond to them, such as Plato's Forms.

Empiricism, however, has been just as bad, says Kant. Although Locke, in his *Essay*, preceded his investigation of what we know by first asking how much we *can* know, he, like the rationalists, went well 'beyond all limits of possible experience', and virtually took it for granted that the external world, the self and causation exist. Hume, following through empiricism's implications, showed that all of these were dubious, since the independent existence and continuity of world and self, and the necessity assumed in causation, are not observable. Other than maths, logic and verbal definitions, then (according to Hume), we know nothing but our perpetually changing experiences.

Thus philosophy in the late 18th century was effectively not even as far advanced as to be in Descartes' position when, having established the thinking 'I', he was trying to escape from solipsism and establish an external world. It was in a yet worse state, since even the self was disintegrated, thanks to Hume – and it was he, famously, who woke Kant from his 'dogmatic slumbers'. Kant realized that if Hume is right, then 'in plain language, this means that there is not and cannot be any such thing as metaphysics at all'.

BREAKING HUME'S FORK–THE SYNTHETIC *A PRIORI*

As Galileo, recanting the earth's rotation in front of the Inquisitors, muttered beneath his breath 'And yet it does move', so Kant seems to have felt 'But we do know, and we do recognize causes and effects as necessary, so we have to start from that assumption.' He uses what he calls a transcendental argument (an argument which, taking for granted that something is the case, asks what has to be possible for it to be so). At the beginning of the *Critique of Pure Reason*, Kant announces that he will examine the faculty of pure reason independently of experience. He declares that the 'proper problem of pure reason is contained in the question: How are *a priori* synthetic judgments possible?' This question sounds dishearteningly technical, but answering it provides a way out of Hume's Fork and of the rationalist/empiricist impasse.

The two prongs to that Fork are: relations of ideas, which are *a priori* (known without experience, and known without possible disproving by experience), and matters of fact which are *a posteriori* (known by means of experience until now, and potentially disprovable by further experience – to deny an *a posteriori* piece of knowledge is not contradictory). Corresponding to each subjective epistemological distinction is an objective metaphysical one about the nature of what is known – that it is either 'necessary' (if true, necessarily true; its opposite being a logical contradiction) or 'contingent' (possibly false; at any rate not contradictory to deny, even if on this occasion it happens to be true).

Kant adds two new distinctions. Treating our knowledge as if it were a series of statements ('judgments'), and taking any judgment to predicate something about its subject, he says there are two sorts of judgment – analytic and synthetic. In an analytic statement, what is predicated is already contained in the subject, because the statement is either one of definition or a tautology (a bachelor is an unmarried man, a rose is a rose). In a synthetic statement, what is predicated says something new about the subject, that is, it is 'ampliative' (a bachelor is free of responsibility, this rose is yellow).

So far it looks as if these three distinctions – *a priori/a posteriori*, necessary/contingent, analytic/synthetic – would be neatly ranged in two separate columns:

How we know something:	*a priori*	*a posteriori*
Objective status of that knowledge:	Necessary	Contingent
Semantic (meaning) status:	Analytic	Synthetic
E.g.	A bachelor is an unmarried man	This bachelor is very happy

Many statements are *a posteriori*, contingent and synthetic. For instance, 'This bachelor is very happy' expresses knowledge gained from experience – knowledge which, even if true in this particular case, may or may not have in fact been true, and may or may not be true of this bachelor on other occasions, and of other bachelors in other cases. Many statements are just as clearly *a priori*, analytic and necessary, for instance 'All triangles have three sides'. Even if there never has been, is not now, and never will be, anything triangular, nonetheless to have been or be a triangle would be to have three sides (given what 'triangle' means).

Ranged in this way, as two exclusive pairs of three, the six distinctions do not do justice to our knowledge, says Kant. There are surely some statements which convey absolute necessity, and yet are *not* analytic (true by virtue of their meaning), but instead ampliative as synthetic statements are.

Most empiricists would say that although knowledge of maths and geometry has to be acquired through teaching, they are each *a priori*, necessary and analytic in the sense that they are applied to our experience rather than being extracted from it, and that no amount of experience can disprove them. Kant agrees that some mathematical and geometrical statements are *a priori*, necessary and analytic, but he contrasts 'Any triangle has three sides' with 'The angles of a triangle add up to 180 degrees', or '7 + 5 = 12'. The latter two statements are *a priori* and necessary, and yet, he says, are synthetic – we have to go outside these concepts to work out the degrees of the angles, or to add up 7 and 5. It is not part of the definition of '7' that adding 5 to 7 makes 12, therefore '7 + 5 = 12' is not analytic but synthetic. Sums involving larger numbers make it more obvious that 'however we might turn and twist our concepts, we could never, by the mere analysis of them, and without the aid of intuition, discover what is the sum'. And yet, if true, the result of the sum is necessarily true, and, synthetic though it is, must be assumed to be true prior to, and irrespective of, all experience.

Maths and geometry are, contends Kant, synthetic *a priori*.

HUME'S MISSING IMPRESSION OF NECESSITY CONNECTION

Kant contrasts two statements: 'All effects have causes' and 'All events have causes'. The first is clearly *a priori*, necessary and analytic. If there were to be any such thing as an effect, it would only count as being an effect in so far as it had a cause. Even if no effects had ever occurred, it would be true that if one did, it must (to correctly be described as an effect) have had a cause. But 'All events have causes' is not analytic (it is not part of the definition of 'event' that an event has a cause), but is, instead, synthetic (giving information about the nature of events). And yet it is also necessarily true, and is assumed to be true prior to, and irrespective of, all experience.

But what entitles us to say this? Is it because so far all events have had causes? Certainly no amount of experience can either prove or disprove that when something happens, something else has caused it to happen. But how do we know that any event will *necessarily* be caused, without observing the necessary connection between cause and effect – unless of course we make an assumption that goes beyond experience's limits?

This was Hume's question, and Kant agrees with Hume that necessity cannot be derived from what we actually perceive in the world. I do not observe the sun causing the once-cold stone to be warm, he says, even though I attribute the stone's warmth to the sun shining on it. But he denies that necessity is just an internal feeling which we extrapolate from repeated experiences. If it were, then, as Hume himself showed, we would only be able to say, even of the most iron necessities (that medium-sized objects fall when dropped, for instance), that they have seemed to be necessary (because we have felt their necessity) up till now, but that they may not be necessary in the future (Hume's problem of induction). 'Experience teaches us that a thing is so and so, but not that it cannot be otherwise'; yet it is clear in some cases that, irrespective of experience, the thing *cannot* be otherwise.

The indispensable

Causation is one of the 'pure *a priori* principles [that] are indispensable for the possibility of experience', says Kant. But Hume's theory makes our belief indirect, caused in the wrong way – caused, not by *necessity*, but instead by our necessitated (and perhaps false) *feeling of necessity*. It is as if we have mistaken 'a subjective necessity (habit) for an objective necessity', which 'in reality [turns out to be] nothing but a bastard of imagination'.

The only alternative to this skewed belief-formation is that the sense of necessity precedes, rather than follows from, our experience. 'Hitherto, it has been assumed that all our knowledge must conform to objects . . . We must . . . make trial whether we may not have more success in the tasks of metaphysics, if we suppose that objects must conform to our knowledge.'

Knowledge that changes in events, and alterations to objects, are caused is 'knowledge [that we have] absolutely independent of all experience' – knowledge that forestalls and shapes experience. Kant is going to show that our perceptions do not correspond to things in the world, but that the things we perceive are, in being perceived, made intelligible by the way in which we perceive them (although how they are in themselves is unknowable). This reversal he calls 'a Copernican revolution', although it sounds the opposite – as if the human observer is being made central again, as we used to be before being demoted to merely circulating. But the point is that we, like the earth, are (cognitively) active, and (perceptually) in motion.

Thus, the opening sentence of the Introduction in the second edition of the *Critique* seems to espouse empiricism: 'There can be no doubt that all our knowledge [sometimes translated as 'cognition'] begins with experience'; but Kant then goes on to say that 'although all our knowledge begins with experience, it does not follow that it all arises out of experience.' In this, often called the first *Critique*, he examines the faculty of pure reason and works out what mental structures must necessarily exist for us to be able to know anything. He is interpreted in many different ways, but no one disputes that he is very difficult.

SENSIBILITY AND UNDERSTANDING

We have two sources of knowledge, says Kant – sensibility (the capacity for sensory experience) and understanding. Through sensibility 'an object is *given* to us' in 'intuition'. Through understanding 'the object is *thought* in relation to that [given] representation'. The word translated as 'intuition' is *anschauung* (the verb *schauen* means 'to look', the prefix *an* means 'at', so *anschauung* means 'a looking at' or 'a view'). According to some interpretations, Kant is referring not to what the mind looks at, but to its activity in looking – the form, not the content – of what

---

- An *intuition* 'is that through which an object is in immediate relation to us'; the representation by which an object is given to us; a sense perception.

- A *concept* relates to objects *'mediately* by means of a feature which several things may have in common'.

- *Sensibility* gives us intuitions: sensed phenomena.

- *Understanding* gives us concepts: objects thought.

- Sensibility and understanding interlock.

Kant criticized Leibniz for arguing that mental representations of secondary qualities are just obscure ideas.

Descartes, Locke and Berkeley called 'ideas', Hume called 'impressions', and 20th-century philosophers would call 'sense data'.

Whether or not Kant uses 'intuition' for a reified sense perception (he sometimes seems to) or for the act of perceiving, he abrogates the rigid demarcation between sensibility and understanding to which both rationalists and empiricists have been prone. Nor will he assume that what we perceptually pick up from the world is either accurately mirrored by our perceptions (primary qualities) or else represented by our perceptions not as it is but in a systematically different guise – coloured, sounding, smelling, tasting a certain way (secondary qualities). He will not presuppose, then, that – apart from the secondary qualities – what we perceive is as we perceive it, or that (secondary qualities excepted) the world is instantly amenable to our perception and 'ready-made' (as Hilary Putnam puts it). Empiricists who make such a presupposition (Locke, for instance) illegitimately go outside our experience. Hume, who doesn't, leaves us in scepticism.

Intellectualizing appearances and sensualizing concepts – how not to

Kant complains that Leibniz 'intellectualized appearances' – that is, Leibniz, like Descartes and Spinoza, considered that our mental representations of secondary qualities are just 'confused and obscure ideas'. It is as if our perceptions of secondary qualities are merely botched and blurred – inadequate as perception because not informing us of the fundamentally mathematical nature of the world, as the so-called 'primary qualities' do.

Conversely, however, Locke (and the other empiricists) 'sensualized' concepts, putting all ideas at the level of sensory experience. Simple ideas (with Locke) or simple impressions (with Hume) supposedly coalesce into complex ideas (with Locke) or, (with Hume), complex impressions that give rise to fainter copies (ideas). But how do the sensed impressions coalesce, and why should they? Empiricism indulges in what has been called 'the Myth of the Given'. It treats sense impressions as self-explanatory, prepackaged for neat assembly like IKEA beds. It does not explain how, in themselves, our sensory impressions can ever constitute more than 'a blooming buzzing confusion' (as William James described a new-born baby's worldview). Most empiricists infringe their own criterion of experience by taking for granted that coherence is intrinsic to the world.

Locke asserted that the mind is a blank sheet on which experience can write. But how would experience's markings even count as doodles, let alone words, unless mind and experience have a language and a script in common? Locke's metaphor makes an unwarranted presupposition – that what writes (experience), what is written upon (the mind), and what is written (impressions/ideas of things) share a symbol system. If they did not, then experience and all that it offers would just be water off a duck's back – it would not be retained or incorporated or developed, or even actually mean anything.

Empiricists tend to neglect, even if they pay lip-service to, the essential fact that a concept relates to objects 'mediately by means of a feature which several things may have in common'. We see an object *as* a table, *as* a dog, *as* a palm-tree. Our perceptions are conceptualized. Kant maintains that there has to be a 'synthesis' of sensibility and understanding in perceiving. 'Without sensibility no object would be given to us, without understanding no object would be thought. Thoughts without content are empty, intuitions without concepts are blind . . . The understanding can intuit nothing, the senses can think nothing. Only through their union can knowledge arise.'

The forms of sensibility – space and time

Kant wants first of all to '*isolate* sensibility' – to take away from it everything conceptual or perceptual – so as to leave nothing but 'pure intuition', the bare structure of experience. This, he thinks, consists of the inner sense of time and the outer sense of space – two inexorably fundamental containers of all our experience.

Arguments for space being an *a priori* intuition

a) 'The representation of space must be presupposed' in order that certain sensations be referred to something outside oneself. 'Outer experience is itself possible at all only through that representation.'

b) Space cannot be derived from experience: 'We can never represent to ourselves the absence of space, though we can quite well think it as empty of objects. It must therefore be regarded as the condition of the possibility of appearances.'

c) We can only represent to ourselves one space. Other spaces (for example between here and the door) are part of this one space, but only as limitations of a unity. A limited space is conceived of as being within space as a whole. Space is a pure intuition. ('Pure intuition . . . contains only the form under which something is intuited.')

The statements a) and b) argue for space being *a priori*, while c) argues for space being an intuition.

Arguments for time being an *a priori* intuition

a) 'Time is not an empirical concept that has been derived from any experience. ... Only on the presupposition of time can we represent to ourselves a number of things as existing at one and the same time (simultaneously) or at different times (successively).'

b) 'We cannot, in respect of appearances in general, remove time itself, though we can quite well think time as void of appearances.'

c) Different times are parts of one and the same time, therefore time (like space) is a pure intuition.

The representation of time underlies all representations whatsoever, 'since all representations, whether they have for their objects outer things or not, belong, in themselves, as determinations of the mind, to our inner state'.

> • Space 'is a necessary *a priori* representation, which underlies all outer intuitions' – the form of outer sense.
>
> • Time 'is a necessary representation that underlies all intuitions' – the form of inner sense.

The categories – the forms of understanding

Space and time are the pure *a priori* intuitions, but we also have pure *a priori* concepts. These frame and organize the actual intuitions that we continually receive, integrating them into specific, causally interacting objects.

Borrowing Aristotle's categories ('kategoria' means an attribute or characteristic that can be predicated of a thing), Kant classifies four sets of three 'pure concepts' (12 in all) which mediate all experience. For Kant, the mind is not, as it is for Locke, a blank sheet of paper inscribed by sensations. It is more like a variegated mould, into which molten experience pours before setting in the differently shaped patterns provided. Or perhaps it could be said that the mind imposes the categories on reality; or that we perceive, and conceive of, reality as if through a grid or through coloured glasses.

TABLE OF CATEGORIES

Of quantity: unity, plurality and totality (including number).

Of quality: reality, negation and limitation (reality combined with negation).

Of relation: substance-and-accident, causality-and-dependence, community or interaction (community of substances reciprocally determining one another).

Of modality: possibility/impossibility, existence/non-existence, necessity/contingency.

Kant borrowed Aristotle's categories, creating four sets of three 'pure concepts'.

Kant himself does not use any of these metaphors, and each may be more misleading than helpful, partly because the mind, for Kant, is both active and passive in its operations. It is not merely a passive recipient of sense-impressions, or these would just be copies of objects. Instead, having been mediated by the forms of inner and outer sense (time and space), our sense impressions are synthesized by the imagination through the 12 pure concepts of the understanding (the categories). 'By *synthesis*, in its most general sense, I understand the act of putting different representations together, and of grasping what is manifold in them in one knowledge,' says Kant. And yet the synthesis of intuition and concept is, as with Hume's Newtonian-force mind, not effected knowingly and consciously – it happens (though see below p.200). It 'is the mere result of the power of imagination, a blind but indispensable function of the soul, without which we should have no knowledge whatsoever.'

According to Descartes, Locke or Hume, the sense impressions ('ideas'; or, for Hume, 'impressions') that I am currently having may, or may not, correspond to (the properties of) an object in the world. I have to judge whether they are an appearance to me of what is really there, or an illusion, since my experience of either would be the same. For Kant, when an object is 'thought', intuition (sensibility) and concept (understanding) have already

PSYCHOLOGIZING KANT

Philosophers are wary of psychologizing Kant, but it is consonant with his substance-and-accident and causality-and-dependence categories that infants very early develop what is called 'object permanence'. By four months, babies will show puzzlement or frustration if, having turned away from some object, they turn back and it has gone. They must have been expecting it to continue being there unobserved, and must already have that 'but it must be somewhere' feeling we have about lost things. The notion of causation seems similarly inbuilt. The most primitive magical thinking is based on it – rain dances, sticking pins in voodoo dolls, cursing enemies, not walking under ladders.

merged. 'It is therefore correct to say that the senses do not err – not because they always judge rightly but because they do not judge at all.'

The most significant categories are substance-and-accident and causality-and-dependence. We apprehend a world of objects that exist over time and causally interact. As said above, Kant denies Hume's solution to how we account for necessary connection: 'The very concept of a cause so manifestly contains the concept of a necessity of connection with an effect and of the strict universality of the rule, that the concept would be altogether lost if we attempted to derive it, as Hume has done, from a repeated association of that which happens with that which precedes, and from a custom of connecting representations.' Hume's extrapolated sense of necessity is 'merely subjective', and *ad hoc*. Kant maintains that, like mathematical propositions, causal judgments 'carry with them necessity, which cannot be derived from experience'.

Schemata

Kant also offers a mechanism to explain 'the *application* of a category to appearances' – a 'transcendental schema' – which, by means of the imagination, mediates between categories and appearances. For he felt that the categories are abstract, and need to be made more concrete in order to be applied in particular cases. The concept 'dog', for instance, 'signifies a rule according to which my imagination can delineate the figure of a four-footed animal in a general manner', without being limited to any dog I actually observe or imagine. The dog schema is, apparently, a likeness both to the pure concept ('dog') and to what is given in sensation. It is at once intellectual and sensory, and (*pace* the empiricists) is not an image but a procedure. Without it, no concept would possess the 'universality' that makes it 'valid' of all its particular instances. If this sounds baffling, that is because it is. Many Kant scholars think that the schemata serve no useful purpose or add anything to the categories. Why should they be any better at being rules for generating suitable images than the categories already are?

What is doing this perceiving and judging?

It may seem odd that Kant makes perceiving primary, and takes the perceiving 'I' (sometimes generalized as 'we') for granted, without

UNITY OF CONSCIOUSNESS

The unity of consciousness, as necessary condition of experience, makes it possible that the 'I' that is now thinking is the same 'I' that was thinking before and will be thinking later. In an important footnote, Kant imagines an elastic ball hitting another elastic ball, in a series, so that each communicates the incremental motion of all the preceding balls to the next. If one substance could similarly transfer to the neighbouring one all previous representations, and the consciousness of them, right down the line, then the last substance would be conscious of all the successive states of the previous ones. 'Yet it would not have been one and the same person in all these states.' In principle, then, there may not be an 'I' as such. That designation 'in no way proves the numerical identity of my subject'.

initially subjecting it to his critique. But that is the point. 'Knowing' is a relationship in which I stand only with respect to phenomena. And 'I', the knower, am not myself part of what is known.

Kant agrees with Hume. 'No fixed and abiding self can present itself in this flux of inner appearances,' he says. But of course, for him, unlike for Hume, a flux of appearances cannot constitute knowledge, which requires that 'representations stand compared and connected'. And, just as he has postulated that appearances are 'gathered' into a synthesis, and mediated by the forms of space and time, and the categories, before being consciously experienced, so he argues for 'the transcendental unity of apperception'. 'Transcendental' here has Kant's sense of 'necessarily presupposed'. As presupposed, 'apperception' (the perception of perceiving) is the grounding and vessel in which perceptions can cohere.

The 'I' is 'already involved in every thought', Kant says; 'the "I think" has to accompany all my representations' or they would not *be* thought, 'or at least would be nothing to me'. But the permanence and unity of the self is not something I experience in intuition (sense experience). The 'representation "I"' is 'in itself completely empty'. 'I' am 'a merely logical subject', only the formal condition of my thoughts and their being mine, not a substratum. I don't deduce, but instead presuppose, 'the simplicity of myself (as soul)'. For synthesis of objects to be possible, there has first to be 'synthesis of apprehension'.

TRANSCENDENTAL IDEALISM AND EMPIRICAL REALISM

For Descartes, the 'I', caught in the act of thinking, is what we are immediately certain of, and know best – the problem being to get beyond subjectivity and seeming to an objective external world. He and Locke are considered Indirect Realists, but Kant accuses them of being 'problematic idealists', and says he is going to turn the game played by idealism against itself. It is experience of sensory stuff that is immediate, he argues; 'inner experience is itself possible only mediately, and only through outer experience'. I don't infer an 'I' from the fact that I think, and 'I have just as little need to resort to inference' in the case of outer objects as I have in regard to myself. Indeed, I have no certainty that 'the consciousness of myself would be even possible apart from things outside me . . . and whether, therefore, I could exist merely as thinking being (that is, without existing in human form).'

Kant calls his position Transcendental Idealism, which amounts, he says, to Empirical Realism. This, he says, is not the 'dogmatic idealism' of Berkeley which 'destroys material things'. Kant may initially sound idealist when saying that how outer objects appear depends on us. But it is only *how* things appear, not their *existence*, that he claims to be mind-dependent. In the *Prolegomena*, he seems to put all our perceptions at the level of secondary qualities, arguing that what we perceive has, in a sense, 'no proper existence outside our representation' any more than heat, colour and taste do.

'The expression "outside us" is', he says 'unavoidably ambiguous... sometimes signifying what *as thing in itself* exists apart from us, and sometimes what belongs solely to outer *appearance*'. And yet there is a non-Cartesian, non-Lockeian, non-Berkeleyian sense in which all objects *are* 'appearances'. For they are how the things-in-themselves (the noumena) appear to us, mediated by pure intuitions and the categories. We never perceive the things-in-themselves (*ding an sich*) as they really are.

FORMAL UNITY OR NOUMENAL SELF?

Kant says that we ourselves introduce 'the order and regularity in the appearances, which we entitle *nature*', and that 'we can know *a priori* of things only what we ourselves put into them'. But of course we don't consciously introduce order and regularity, or knowingly instil space, time and the categories into things. The synthesizing of experience is not itself experienced but, as with Hume's 'principles of association', activated in advance of perceiving, without our knowing that we activate it; and not by the empirical self we are aware of, but by our transcendental self. But then doesn't Kant's view of cognition come to much the same as Hume's – a congeries of mental activities passively manipulated by 'the current of nature'?

No, because although Kant objects to the Cartesian notion of a mental substance, he himself does what he accuses Descartes of doing – 'steps beyond the world of sense . . . into the field of noumena'. He sometimes hints that the transcendental self is also *transcendent*, or that, if it is not, we have to take it to be. 'I have no knowledge of myself *as I am* [my italics] but merely as I appear to myself'. 'We designate the subject . . . only transcendentally, without noting in it any quality whatsoever – in fact without knowing anything of it either by direct acquaintance or otherwise.' But that leaves open the possibility that there is something that could, potentially, be known – that while, on this (the phenomenal) side of experience, the transcendental subject constitutes the barely-sensed unifying funnel of consciousness, on the other (noumenal) side beyond it there stretches a noumenal self. Could I therefore be not only something beyond my own knowledge, but also – insofar as this unknowable self is exempt from space, time, substance and causation – also free?

THE ANTINOMIES

That we are free, and that we are subject to causation, is the paradox in one of Kant's four Antinomies. Each of these is a pair of contradictory statements, which, says Kant, is engendered by reason getting exorbitant and trying to think beyond the bounds of experience, using 'the concept – itself only an idea [that is, not one of Kant's structuring concepts] – of the world-whole'. Each Antinomy has a thesis and an antithesis, which, between them, apparently state the only two possible, if mutually exclusive, truths on the matter:

Kant was famously solitary, yet was dubbed the 'King in Königsberg' for his importance in the city's literary and artistic circles.

1   *Thesis:* That the world has a beginning in time, and limits in space;
   Antithesis: that it doesn't have either;

2   *Thesis:* That nothing exists except things composed of simple parts, or the simple parts themselves;
   Antithesis: that there are no simple parts in the world;

3   *Thesis:* That, as well as causality in accordance with natural laws, there is a causality of freedom;
   Antithesis: that there is no freedom, and everything is subject to natural law;

4   *Thesis:* That there belongs to the world, either as its part or as its cause, an absolutely necessary being;
   Antithesis: that no absolutely necessary being exists in the world, or outside it as its cause.

Kant argues both sides of each Antinomy. In the end, he says, it is as if both sides are left exhausted rather than injured, and will perhaps recognize 'the futility of their quarrel' and 'part good friends'.

Not-free but free

Yet, with the third Antinomy, he may perhaps mean that both the contradictory propositions are true – the antithesis being true of phenomena, the thesis true of noumena (therefore ultimately true). Kant is trying to work out what has to be the case for us to have the experience and knowledge that we have, and surely we cannot, in practice, not see ourselves as occupying this paradoxical position. Even those who say that free will is just an illusion feel (at least) that they have incessantly to make decisions (however illusory).

The empirical self is part of the appearances. It is bound by the laws of nature and the pull of desires. I discover it empirically along with anything else I experience, through observing my behaviour at particular times, and over time. I can get to learn, often ruefully, about my character ('I'm not very generous, am I?'), and act accordingly ('To counter my stinginess, I'll make a standing order to Oxfam'; 'Since I tend to be late, I'll set my clocks five minutes early').

But of course I don't navigate life by making predictions about myself. It would be facetious to say: 'Don't bother to bring a menu. What I've always had till now is the leek and potato soup, so I can only assume that I'll have it this time.' There are, admittedly, ways it makes sense to say 'I'll probably end up marrying him', but you wouldn't just find that you'd arrived at the registry office.

I can 'know' that my decisions are caused by the beliefs and desires that have been moulded by my genes, conditioning and habits, but in the thick of life I also 'know' that I am deciding, and responsible for my decisions. Not only is that how it feels; I am in fact unable not to decide. I am simultaneously not-free and free, and I can't duck out of this freedom, which is inescapable. I am, as Sartre said, 'condemned to be free'.

GOD

Kant had earned fame for *The Only Possible Argument in Support of a Demonstration of the Existence of God* (written in his pre-critical period in 1763) which attacked the Ontological Argument and the Argument from Design, although concluded that God necessarily exists (the thesis of the fourth Antinomy). In the first *Critique*, he demolishes three arguments for God's existence.

1) The Ontological Argument, used by Descartes (see p.43), says that God's existence is entailed by the very idea of God. He is, by definition, a perfect being. Not to exist would be to lack a perfection, and thus to not be a perfect being. To say that God does not exist would, therefore, be to contradict the very concept you have just enunciated. Kant replies that there is 'already a contradiction' in surreptitiously making the concept of existence part of a concept before demonstrating that the concept of which it is part is anything more than possible. You cannot validly argue 'from the logical possibility of concepts to the real possibility of things'. Existence is not a predicate. To predicate of a thing is to say what properties it has *if it exists*: 'Emily is studious', 'Emily is pretty', 'Emily is deceitful' can only be jointly or individually true if Emily exists; to say that she 'is' or 'has existence' is not to ascribe her an extra property in addition to the other properties she has. Nor could existence be one of the properties included in the properties that constitute perfection. 'If we attempt to think existence through the pure category alone, we cannot specify a single mark distinguishing it from mere possibility ... We can no more extend our stock of [theoretical] insight by mere ideas, than a merchant can better his position by adding a few noughts to his cash account.' Also, every judgment must be either analytic or synthetic. The Ontological Argument is illegitimately both; existence being (allegedly) part of the definition of 'God', yet also added to it.

2) The Cosmological (First Cause) Argument covertly presupposes the Ontological Argument, so as to include God's perfections. In any case, to argue that God is self-caused and a necessary being is to apply the principle that everything must have a cause (a principle that is only validly applicable within the sensible world)

In his Critique of Pure Reason, *Kant demolished the three main arguments for the existence of God.*

to the sensible world as a whole, thus claiming to think beyond the limits of phenomena. (Hume argues similarly.)

3) The Physico-Theological Argument (Argument from Design) appeals to the notion that the world's intricate workings necessarily imply a designer. But it relies on the Cosmological Argument, which in turn relies on the Ontological Argument, to 'prove' God's being as necessary and perfect. The most it could actually prove would be 'an architect of the world who is always very much hampered by the adaptability of the material in which he works, not a creator of the world to whose idea everything is subject'.

NOUMENA – WHAT AND WHERE?

Schopenhauer compared the noumena (the things-in-themselves, as they exist apart from space, time and the categories) to Plato's Forms. But Plato said that the Forms (intelligible concepts) are the only things we can know, while about sensible things we can merely have opinions. Kant, however, insists that the phenomena are known, and the noumena unknowable. Instead of mistakenly reifying noumena into positive things, we should conceive of noumena merely negatively. They are reality as we, whose access to objects is always sensuously mediated, do not perceive it.

Still, the inevitable question is: Where are the noumena? One interpretation is that they are (like the Forms) nowhere, because they are outside space, time, substantiality and causation. Another (and perhaps consonant) interpretation is that the noumena are all around us – the trees, rivers, houses, streets and tables are noumena but perceived as phenomena. If we can't perceive the things-in-themselves, but only the appearances of them, can it be non-heretically said that in a sense the noumena (which are immanent and surround us) *are* what we perceive, it is just that we do not perceive them as they *really* are? And do other creatures also have the inner sense of time and outer sense of space, and apply schemata when recognizing that another creature is of the same type as they are (a dog or octopus) or distinguishing it as a predator?

THE CAPITULATING FOX

The soul, free will, immortality and God – all are concepts that are, strictly speaking, unthinkable because they are outside the remit of experience and meaning. About each of them Kant says, in the first *Critique*, that he has 'therefore found it necessary to deny *knowledge*, in order to make room for *faith*', rather as the early Wittgenstein would later exhort us to 'pass over in silence' the unempirical. But in the second *Critique*, he 'postulates' that what he previously declared unknowable may be true. We navigate our moral lives, he says, under the assumption that there is (or may be) a good Creator of a purposeful world in which the immortal soul can, in 'an endless progress', make itself holy, and in which it truly would be free. If true, these postulates present the cosmos as good and meaningful, and make the huge structure of his metaphysics, ethics and aesthetics beautifully fit together.

Nietzsche compared Kant to a fox that has cleverly broken out of its cage, and then loses his way and returns to it. But he didn't quite go back, and in any case he has broken the cage for others. The gap he thought faith could seal has never really been filled.

Key points

- Kant realized that neither rationalism nor empiricism can account for if, or how, we know about the world. Both leave us stuck in our 'ideas'.

- That we do have knowledge has to be taken for granted, so Kant wanted to work out what needs to be the case for the gap between perceiving and things perceived to be bridged.

- He effected a 'Copernican revolution' – postulating that, rather than our knowledge conforming to things, instead things are fitted to what we can know.

- Knowledge arises from experience, but, rather than being blank slates on which experience writes, our minds structure what we perceive.

- We don't discover *empirically* that the world is temporally and spatially ordered. We have to experience everything as being situated in space and time.

- In perceiving, there is not a problem of first sensing, then conceptualizing. Objects are sensed and thought in a 'synthesized manifold' under 12 forms of understanding (the categories).

- The categories are conditions of our thinking; necessary if we are to have the knowledge and experience that we actually have.

- We see, not a confused flux, but discrete objects, because of the category of substance-and-accident; we don't discover, but presuppose, causal regularity; and so on.

- Kant calls his position transcendental idealism, which, he says, amounts to empirical realism.

- It is realist in so far as it embraces a reality outside us, but idealist in that, however good our science, we will only ever be able to perceive and understand phenomena (appearances), not the unknowable things-in-themselves.

- The 'I' is not what we know best; it is, and may perhaps only be, the presupposed framework of experience.

- The soul, like free will, God and immortality, is placed beyond knowledge; but the concept of free will, at least, is necessary to the way we are and live.

Chapter 10

Immanuel Kant (1724–1804): Moral Philosophy

M oral philosophers such as Aristotle and Hume start with human nature, and treat morality as a benign public institution designed to satisfy our properly realized desires. The objectivity they appeal to is that of human psychology and social custom. Virtue is taken to be the behaviour best suited to attaining and maintaining what we truly want (flourishing, happiness); and the virtues they analyse are the accepted virtues of their time.

Kant in his stern, purist way, goes deeper. In the *Groundwork of the Metaphysics of Morals*, he announces that, rather than 'doing anthropology', he aims to 'seek out and establish *the supreme principle of morality*' – the principle which holds not just 'under the contingent conditions of humanity' but 'for all *rational beings as such . . . with absolute necessity*'. 'All human virtue in circulation is small change – it is a child who takes it for real gold,' he writes. Morality too must be critiqued.

As someone of intensely religious background, he recognizes morality's vertiginously opposite extremes – spanning 'the starry heavens above me and the moral law within', freedom and compulsoriness. Unlike social laws, which are local and public, the demands of moral rules are hyper-objective and universal, yet are addressed to the individual conscience, which, in unknowable privacy, alone can answer them.

Kant begins with, and focuses on, the moral agent – not as experiencer and emoter, or as social citizen, but as rational being. He acknowledges that, being 'rational but finite', we necessarily want happiness, but, he argues, happiness is 'an indeterminate concept': everyone wants it, no one knows what it is they actually want. Riches, knowledge, a long life, health – only omniscience would tell us which, if any, of them will make us happy. Where, in practice, anyone finds their happiness 'comes down

Kant's moral philosophy focuses on the rational being as a moral agent.

to the particular feeling of pleasure and displeasure in each [person], and, even within one and the same subject, to needs that differ as this feeling changes'.

Reason could not, Kant argues, be designed to achieve happiness, which is, rather, the product of instinct, dependent on circumstance and character, and unfree. In morality, reason, far from being 'slave to the passions', should rule.

FREE WILL VERSUS DETERMINISM

Kant says that the only way to make sense of the world is by seeing everything in it as being subject to cause and effect; if so, how can we see ourselves as exempt from causation and having choice in, and

Hume believed that freedom was merely the absence of obstacles to carrying out our desires, but Kant argued this was a 'wretched subterfuge'.

responsibility for, our actions? How could we be different from everything else in the universe?

Responding to the problem of determinism, Hume says that just as we do not observe causal necessity in nature, but are compelled to assume it, so, in the case of human behaviour, we have to assume that certain motives inevitably precede certain actions, including our own: freedom consists merely in having no impediments to carrying out the desires that we are (apparently) caused to have. Kant calls Hume's compatibilist solution 'a wretched subterfuge', 'petty word-jugglery' and superficial, but agrees that, if we are not to abandon common-sense, we can find 'no true contradiction . . . between freedom and natural necessity in the same human actions'. And his transcendental idealism gives him an opt-out clause that is unavailable to Hume. Kant argues that we do not garner a notion of causal necessity from experience, but that experience is already primed and imbued with the category of 'causation-and-dependence'. Since it is one of the categories we impose on the world, it is therefore not an intrinsic part of reality, the true nature of which is unknowable. It is therefore possible that 'I', as well as constituting the 'formal unity' which gives coherence to my experience, may be part of the noumena, to which causality does not apply.

The agent, Kant says, 'regards himself at the same time as . . . *appearance*', embroiled in the causality of the sensory world, and as noumenon, 'as pure intelligence . . . that cannot be temporally determined'.

CONSCIOUSNESS OF FREEDOM

Tantalisingly, Kant leaves it an open question whether we really have free will or whether it is just 'a postulate' that we have to assume for practical and moral purposes. In the *Groundwork*, he says that 'The concept of the intelligible [noumenal] world is ... only *a point of view* which reason finds itself constrained to adopt outside appearances *in order to conceive itself as practical*'. In the *Critique of Practical Reason*, he suggests that in some way the phenomenal and noumenal intersect. But whether or not we do have free will, 'man actually finds in himself a power which distinguishes him from all other things – and even from himself so far as he is affected by objects'.

Kant offers an illustration of the way in which we know (or 'know') that we're free: a man feels that he will die if he doesn't have sex, and goes to the brothel. He is told that he is free to enter, but that, once he has satisfied the urges that he insists are irresistible, he will be hung on the gallows erected outside. His response is totally predictable. Suddenly he won't after all die if he doesn't have sex, since he will die if he does have it. He leaves.

But, says Kant, if the state's ruler orders him, on pain of death by hanging, to give false witness against an innocent man in a trial, then he knows that it *is* possible to conquer his love of life – although he may not in fact do so – and that indeed he *should*. 'He judges, therefore, that he can do something because he is aware that he ought to do it, and he cognises freedom within him which, without the moral law, would have remained unknown to him.' He recognizes that he is free by realizing that he is bound. By a beautifully self-fulfilling prophecy, we are free by virtue of thinking we are free . . . and bound.

Free and bound

To be free is, paradoxically, to recognize and obey the moral law. By obeying it, you are freer, according to Kant, than someone compelled by desire, emotion, fear, or the hope of reward (including reward in Heaven). Compulsions of those sorts make a person 'subject only to the law of nature – the law of his own needs'. Whereas in obeying the categorical self-command, he 'is subject only to laws which are made by himself and yet are universal'.

If we were perfectly rational, we would see ourselves as part of the noumenal world, and want to be moral. But being also part of the phenomenal world, and creatures of inclination, the moral law is something which we have to obey. 'This "I ought" is properly an "I will" which holds necessarily for every rational being provided that reason in him is practical without any hindrance. For beings who, like us, are affected also by sensibility – that is, by motives of a different kind – and who do not always act as reason by itself would act, this necessity is expressed as an "I ought."' When our actions proceed from the moral law, what ought to be the case coincides with what is.

NO PSYCHOLOGICAL INCENTIVE

We are conscious of freedom as 'an ability to follow the moral law with an unyielding disposition', says Kant. But how do we acquire this disposition, what makes us want to acquire it, and what is it in aid of?

Kant does not appeal to the 'usefulness' and 'agreeableness' of moral qualities, as Hume does, and has no prompting psychological mechanism equivalent to Hume's 'sympathy'. He scorns the 'amiable'. Just as his metaphysics sets out to examine pure reason, so his moral philosophy examines pure *practical* reason, in pursuing the question of how morality can be founded in reason and necessity, independently of what people happen to want. He considers to be merely 'coquettish' any ethics that offers external inducements to morality, such as a feeling

---

PRACTICAL REASON

'Practical reason' (a term first used by Aristotle) is reasoning about what to do. Kant agrees with Hume that it tends to be merely instrumental, a servicer of desire. 'Pure practical reason', though, is reason that produces 'consciousness of mastery over one's inclinations' and creates its own laws in accordance with duty, enabling me to act independently of what I (inadvertently) want. Still, just as the empirical and the noumenal self are one, so pure reason and practical reason are the same faculty (reason), 'distinguished merely in its application',

> 'Now an action done from duty must wholly exclude the influence of inclination, and along with inclination every object of the will; so there is nothing left able to determine the will except objectively the *law*, and subjectively *pure reverence* for this practical law, and therefore the maxim of obeying this law even to the thwarting of all my inclinations'.
>
> Immanuel Kant, *Groundwork of the Metaphysics of Morals*

of compassion, the desire for happiness or a good reputation. A good will is '*self-produced* by a rational concept', for which the only 'becoming expression' is 'reverence'; and nothing that 'subserves' inclination, only what 'overwhelms' it, can be an object of reverence.

Not even an inclination to kindness has moral worth. Benevolent people usually enjoy being benevolent, he says. Having a generous disposition is just a matter of luck, and is liable to change if circumstances do. Besides, what is conventionally seen as good (gifts of character, talent or fortune) can easily become bad if not resulting from a good will. The person who is by nature cold-hearted, yet manages to behave well, not from inclination but from duty, is more virtuous.

A good will

But then what does virtue consist in? What are our inclinations being overwhelmed for, if not for compassionate actions? What actually *is* good? Kant seems to have it the other way round: reason is designed to produce a good will, which is the only thing in the world, 'or even out of it', that can be 'taken as good without qualification'. And to act out of a 'good will' is to act out of 'duty'.

But duty to do what? What is the 'good will'? These concepts seem circular.

Kant side-steps Hume's is/ought problem – the difficulty of shifting us from how things are in the natural world to how we should act on them, and how they should be in the world we make. For Kant, morality, rather than a set of flat descriptive statements that require correspondent facts, is an active, prescribing law – and not a determinate law but one

Kant states that morality is an active and prescriptive law that is perpetually made and remade.

that is perpetually made, and remade, by each moral agent legislating to themselves.

We spin moral values out of our own reasoning. The content of the moral law, in fact, is up to us – but not in the Subjectivist's manner. Kant wants to reach beyond varying and ephemeral social convention to a far more cosmically objective moral law, which, for that very reason, is both far more various, and far more specific and personal, than accepted morality. It is subjectively formulated each time I, the rational agent, issue my self-command, but, because that self-command takes everyone else into account, it is not just issued to me but is objective and universal.

THE CATEGORICAL MORAL IMPERATIVE

I work out the moral law each time I am about to do anything (and it's likely that, as with Sartre, this really *is* anything – boiling an egg, cleaning my teeth, the most trivial action). I look at the maxim (rule, principle) under which my putative action would fall, and ask if I would be willing for an action of that description to be one that everyone *had to do*. 'I ought never to act except in such a way that I can also will that my maxim should become a universal law.' Where I can't, the maxim or action 'is to be rejected, and that not because of a prospective loss to you or even to others, but because it cannot fit as a principle into a possible enactment of universal law'.

It is only reasonable, in fact, for me to act on a maxim that I could be happy to legislate for everyone else to do. Why, (Kant is asking), should an action be right for me when it is wrong for others? If it is right for me, it must be right for anyone else. After all, I am one person among many, and why should I have special privileges? What's the big deal about me? I cannot, in all reason, do something unless I am prepared for everyone else to do it too. If I would hate for the action I am about to do to be one that was generally done, on what grounds am I entitled to make an exception for myself?

Therefore: 'I ought never to act except in such a way that I can also will that my maxim should become a universal law.' Where I can't, the maxim or action 'is to be rejected, and that not because of a prospective loss to you or even to others, but because it cannot fit as a principle into a possible enactment of universal law'.

For example, 'I can indeed will to lie, but I can by no means will a universal law of lying; for by such a law there could properly be no promises at all, since it would be futile to profess a will for future action to others who would not believe my profession or who, if they did so over-hastily, would pay me back in like coin; and consequently my maxim, as soon as it was made a universal law, would be bound to annul itself.' Someone who 'asks permission' to think about possible exceptions to telling the truth is already 'potentially a liar' and self-contradicting; for he shows that he 'reserves exceptions for himself' and 'does not recognize truthfulness as a duty in itself'.

...Versus hypothetical imperatives

The question of whether I can will my action to be a universal law, despite what Kant intends, often sounds as if it does after all take consequences into account. It is, however, meant to be a thought experiment that tests, not for consequences, but for consistency – and that will result in a self-command that is categorical (unbendingly exigent). Kant contrasts this 'categorical imperative' with the usual 'hypothetical [if-based] imperative' that you give others or yourself – if-based because depending on what you want. 'Stop at those lights (if you don't want to break the law or risk causing an accident)'; 'Work hard (if you want to pass your exams, which in turn will help you get a good job or make you happy)'; 'Do good (if you want to get to Heaven)'. In true morality, commands are categorical, because they don't depend on what you want now, or what you want to achieve. The command, the action, the good will – all are insulated from desire, feeling, consequences, the future. Yet at the same time as being self-contained and individual, they embrace the whole of humanity.

What the categorical moral imperative is not

Kant is not, like an infuriating school-teacher, asking 'How would you like it if everyone else did that?' He – or rather the moral agent on the brink of action – is not concerned to ask about, or ascertain, the possible consequences of the action, but whether doing it is consistent and fair. Am I making a special exception for myself? Or am I happy that anyone – indeed everyone – else does as I am about to do?

> ## MORAL THEORIES
>
> Teleological moral theories (for example Utilitarianism): what is good, and what makes an action good, is what it achieves, for example, increasing the amount of happiness in the world, and preventing suffering. Morality has the telos (purpose) of promoting happiness (or some such goal), including the moral agent's.
>
> Deontological moral theories (for example Kant's): what is good, and what makes an action good, is that the action is done out of duty (deon). Its consequences are irrelevant.

Nor is the categorical imperative simply a more grandiose version of 'Do as you would be done by'. In a footnote, Kant calls that Golden Rule 'trivial' and claims it to be 'merely derivative from our principle', because it doesn't contain the ground of duties to oneself or others. It would allow for the man who says 'I wouldn't want to be helped myself, so I have no need to help others' or for the convicted criminal to demand that the judge, who wouldn't like to be jailed, should therefore not send him to jail. The categorical imperative is nothing to do with what we want, or how we would like to be treated ourselves. It goes beyond individual desires to the reasoned-out view of what a desirable society would be. The purely self-interested action cancels itself out as a general rule to be applied. Reason 'anuls itself'. Whereas any action that *anyone* does ought to be capable of satisfactorily being made compulsory for *everyone*.

ONLY GOOD WILL MATTERS

It is not enough to do an action which happens to accord *with* duty: the action must be done *out of* duty. Even when an act is done according to duty, but not from duty, and instead from some other motive (out of self-interest, perhaps, or to seem honourable) then, because it isn't done from duty, it has no moral worth. Kant's example is the shopkeeper, who is scrupulously honest to his customers, but whose honesty is merely due to prudence, and would be abandoned if he could be dishonest with total impunity.

Thus the 'good will' is not good because of its effects but 'through its willing alone – that is, good in itself'. The usefulness or fruitfulness of what it accomplishes 'can neither add to, nor subtract from [its] value'. And the same for what we do. 'What is essentially good in the action consists in the mental disposition, let the consequences be what they may.'

COMMONSENSE

Kant says that he is merely articulating philosophically the way everyone implicitly reasons anyway (he was particularly thinking of his uneducated, pious parents). 'All moral concepts have their seat and origin in reason completely *a priori*, indeed in the most ordinary human reason just as much as in the most highly speculative', all the more so since they can't be derived from empirical, merely contingent, knowledge. Reason itself, however, can help us to quibble with the strict laws of duty, adapting them to our own desires and interpretations. So philosophical clarification is necessary – it helps us to use reason properly.

It is indicative that as societies become more sophisticated, they tend to appeal (in law and still more in day-to-day morality) to the motives, rather than the effects, of actions.

Formulations of the categorial imperative

It would be odd if these were intended to be different ways of saying the same thing; more likely the first formulation is meant to entail the others:

1) 'Act only on that maxim through which you can at the same time will that it should become a universal law.'
(This is very similar to 2, but emphasizes that laws of nature are about agents and what they cause.)

2) 'Act as if the maxim of your action were to become through your will a universal law of nature.'
(Very similar to 1, but emphasizes that laws of nature are about effects.)

3) 'Act in such a way that you always treat humanity, whether in your own person or in the person of any other, never simply as a means, but always at the same time as an end.'

KANT'S EXAMPLES:

a) The would-be suicide: the very same feeling – self-love – that has the function of promoting the continuation of life would prompt its destruction, and that is a contradiction. This course of action 'could not subsist as a system of nature'.

b) The empty promiser asks for a loan, intending not to keep his promise to repay it, but he should 'transform the demand of self-love into a universal law'. He will then realize that, if everyone made empty promises, 'it would make promising, and the very purpose of promising, itself impossible, since no one would believe he was being promised anything, but would laugh at utterances of this kind as empty shams'.

c) The lazy talented man sees that there could in fact be a system of nature in which everyone just devoted themselves to enjoyment 'like the South Sea Islanders' (whom Kant often takes to exemplify self-indulgent sybarites), but he 'cannot possibly will that this should become a universal law of nature or should be implanted in us as such a law by a natural instinct'. (Kant could be accused of tendentiousness here, and racism!)

d) The flourishing neglecter of others can afford to say, 'Let everyone be as happy as he himself, or providence, makes him', but a will that decided thus 'would be in conflict with itself', since the flourishing man may at some point need love and sympathy himself. (Schopenhauer objected that this is prudential, not a watertight moral argument, but, if so, that is not Kant's intention.)

Kant views the four examples in the light of this particular formulation. For example, the false promiser is 'intending to make use of another man *merely as a means* to an end he does not share.' The man thus used 'cannot possibly agree with my way of behaving to him, and so cannot himself

Kant was small, with a large head, one shoulder higher than the other, and very bright blue eyes.

share the end of the action'.

Sometimes, in quoting this formulation of the categorical moral imperative, people leave out the 'simply'. But it is important that Kant is being practical. Most of us spend our time using people as a means, with their agreement, and engaging to have ourselves used as a means in whatever job we do. The point is that no one is to be treated *merely* as a means. If you take a taxi to Paddington station, the driver is perfectly happy to be the means of getting you there, and you are entitled to use her as such. If, though, she suddenly collapses with a heart-attack, and thus ceases to be a means to your reaching the station, you are not entitled to just hop out and summon the next taxi that comes along. You are obliged to treat the taxi-driver as an end in herself. You must ring for an ambulance, ensure that she gets to hospital – and miss your train.

4) 'Act in such a way that you are by your maxims in every case a legislating member in the universal kingdom of ends.'

Kant explicitly denies that promoting or attaining happiness is the goal of morality. Yet this fourth formulation gestures beyond the individual's good will and towards setting dutiful actions in a framework of beneficial consequences at a social level.

At a more metaphysical level, he suggests in the second *Critique* that struggling to attain a good will is perhaps not just an isolated and purely rational burden but is in accordance with the world as it really is – a good and meaningful cosmos designed by a good God who desires our ultimate bliss. If we are not to degrade the moral law by seeing it as 'lenient' and 'conformed to our convenience', we have to account for the 'endless progress' that the soul must undergo before becoming 'holy'. Therefore, we have to assume that each rational being has a 'personality' that continues endlessly: an immortal soul.

We should, says Kant, take the existence of a good God and the immortality of the soul at least as 'postulates' of 'pure practical reason'.

CONSISTENCY

Kant is convinced that 'human reason, with this compass [the categorical moral imperative] in hand, is well able to distinguish, in all cases that present themselves, what is good or evil, right or wrong'. When we act immorally, he says, we 'only take the liberty of making an exception to [the universal law] for ourselves (or even just for this once) to the advantage of our inclination'. But if we weighed it all up from one and the same point of view – reason – 'we should find a contradiction in our own will, the contradiction that a certain principle should be objectively necessary as a universal law and yet subjectively should not hold universally but should admit of exceptions'.

Don't see yourself as exempt from the rules you apply to everyone else; don't treat yourself as uniquely entitled. Lopsided inconsistency is certainly a feature of psychopathy: the man who has murdered his family with an axe is outraged if someone treads on his toe. But similarly, at the everyday level, the tenant who has defrauded you is full of moral indignation if you don't return his book.

The other person points out, 'You expect x, and disapprove of y, but you yourself are y-ing right now'. To which the invariable response is: 'But that's *different*.' It rarely is.

OBJECTIONS
1) Consequences and moral conflicts
    a) There are times when intuitively we feel (though 'feel' would obviously not hold water with Kant) that the consequences of an action outweigh its intrinsic moral wrongness – in fact turn what

would normally be wrong into the right thing to do. The French novelist Benjamin Constant wrote to Kant that to take the duty of truth-telling unconditionally would make any society impossible. If a murderer pursuing your friend asked you whether or not he was in your house (and he was), surely it would be right to lie. But Kant's reply is that if you can't be silent you should tell the truth. He reiterates the categorical imperative, yet also sounds inconsistently consequentialist – a lie 'always harms another, even if not another individual, nevertheless humanity generally, in as much as it makes the source of right unusable'.

b) It is sometimes objected that Kant's moral agent is too afraid of getting his hands dirty. In the lying-to-the-murderer essay, he says that if you told what you thought was a lie, and your friend, who had in fact left the house, met the murderer in the street and was killed by him, you could 'by right' be prosecuted for being instrumental in your friend's death. Whereas if you tell the truth and the murderer murders your friend in your house, then it is not you who, 'strictly speaking, *does* the harm... instead an accident *causes* the harm.' Kant is not of course being cynically prudential here. He is concerned to show how the noumenal self is immune from the phenomenal fray. But that itself, for the ordinary moralist, might seem to selfishly prioritize the moral agent's soul, at whatever cost to others.

c) Kant doesn't really cater for occasions when moral principles clash, or when no good action is possible, and it's necessary to choose the least bad.

2) Consequences and conscientiousness

Even where no transgression of the moral law is in question, it can surely only be said of an action that its motives matter, and its consequences don't, by a third-person observer, not by the action's perpetrator. In advance of acting, the good-willed agent must conscientiously intend to alleviate suffering, tell the difficult truth, or whatever the action involves, rather than just basking in the goodness of their maxim and motives. If they are concerned only to act from duty, rather than in order to achieve some worthwhile end, they are overly self-preoccupied

Benjamin Constant argued that unconditional truth-telling would make society impossible.

and/or not sufficiently wedded to the duty, and to what it entails and consists in doing; which necessarily includes the action's goal. Only afterwards, if at all, is the moral agent entitled to say that it doesn't matter that the action failed or had bad consequences. Before acting, the virtuous agent must envisage and whole-heartedly embrace the action's purpose – or it would not really *be* their purpose in doing it. Their motives would not be whole-heartedly pure. So only the observer, and not the agent, can properly say, on a particular occasion, that a good will, or an action, 'is good, not as a means to some further end, but in itself'.

3) Impersonal approach

Kant's is a philosophy of equality, which makes all of us rational members of a moral community to whom the moral law impartially applies. But in that very virtue of rendering us the same lies one of Kant's problems: he talks as if we are, and should see ourselves as, indistinguishable ciphers, whereas surely we aren't the same, and different circumstances do make a difference. We take on roles which we are then obliged to fulfil, and which entail that we don't, and shouldn't, simply ask 'Could I will for everyone and anyone to do what I am about to do?' Instead we (surely rightly) ask 'Could I will for any mother/sister/teacher/friend to do this?' Admittedly, he does mention *types of duty*, but the categorical imperative allows no room for adjustment. Even to save a life we may not lie. Post-Kantian deontologists occasionally allow for some flexibility, but clearly the more bespoke and personalized an action's maxim is made, the more room there is for partiality and self-interest. ('Let it be a universal law that anyone who feels as sad and lustful as I do should have an affair with their friend's husband.') Tailor-made maxims would reduce the force of the moral law and of its application. They would precisely abrogate the whole point of Kant's consistent, fair, equal, rational system.

If too impersonal, however, Kant's system incurs the same criticism that is often levelled at Utilitarianism: that you are committed to, for instance, saving the most worthy and socially useful travellers on the sinking boat in preference to your own children.

4) Feelings and virtuousness

Linked to this is the objection that Kant is arid, that he undervalues feeling at the expense of reason.

There are surely moral feelings as well as moral actions. Arguably, it is wrong not to feel grief, or even anger, on certain occasions. Aristotle may not be a moral purist, but there is something more than merely attractive in his notion that virtue consists in being spontaneously inclined to act in certain ways which have become part of one's natural repertoire. Is

Kant believed every nation should have a republican constitution to protect citizens' freedoms and ensure their equality.

SOLITARY LIFE

It is indicative that Kant lived a solitary life and had no dependents (except, for a time, his siblings). He was conscientious in helping his family when his father died, and financially generous to his siblings; but he avoided having much to do with them – he may, in adulthood, have felt that they and he no longer had anything in common. When, in his old age, his sister came to nurse him, he was embarrassed by her 'simplicity', and refused to let her eat at the same table. On a page of an emotional letter that he had received from his brother, he wrote 'All morality consists in the derivation of an action from the idea of the subject, *not* from *feeling*.'

it merely aesthetic prejudice that makes us prefer the blithely generous person to the person who is generous through gritted teeth?

Kant is right that warm-heartedness is unreliable, and that some people are cursed with curmudgeonly characters, but he sometimes neglects the importance of character-building which Aristotle and Virtue Ethics (Aristotle's contemporary reincarnation) emphasize. Kant would obviously agree as to the value of building up good habits, and morality's concern with self-fashioning, but perhaps there is something too stop-and-start about his moral system as expressed in the *Groundwork*. Is life just a series of moral decisions? Actions are not so much interferences in the course of things as expressions and manifestations of ourselves. Deciding whether or not to lie works well as an example of a categorical imperative, but what about loving? Love, Kant could reply, is more what you do than what you feel.

5) The good society

What is all this rational decision-making in aid of if it doesn't deal with human well-being and suffering? Surely individual desires have to come in somewhere, and also a desirable (in both senses) society. Kant's fourth formulation of the categorical moral imperative seems to allow for that – and although his ethics is apolitical, he wrote about his idea of a good society in his later years. Every nation should have a republican constitution, he argues in his essay 'Towards Perpetual Peace', since that is the only sort that ensures its citizens their individual freedoms, a common legislation and equality. He was not keen on democracy, though.

6) The categorical moral imperative is only prohibiting and negative. It offers guidance less on what to do than on what not to do.

By the same token, however, it avoids the hubris of Utilitarianism, in which, because promoting the greatest happiness of the greatest number is the only motive for action, you are encouraged to violate human rights, and sacrifice the few for the many; a devotion to consequences which is liable to have disastrous consequences itself.

7) Noumenal and phenomenal

Heartening as Kant's model of the noumenal self is, it is hard to see how it can work. Supposedly, practical reason enables the will to rise above causation (the ordinary causation of desire and inclination) but how does the noumenal interact with the phenomenal self? And wouldn't the interaction entail causal relations, from noumenal to phenomenal, even though causation is strictly confined to phenomena?

'Will is a kind of causality,' says Kant, which is both 'in accordance with the laws of nature' and 'itself free from all laws of nature'. But he doesn't explain how.

8) Moral luck

The watertight appraisal of action that Kant advocates – that an action be judged purely on the basis of its agent's motives, irrespective of its results – would be psychologically and practically almost impossible. There is, after all, what Bernard Williams calls 'moral luck' – whether an action has good or bad consequences inevitably affects its reception. For instance an episode of careless driving may or may not cause an accident, but only if it does will the driver be punished. Gauguin's desertion of his wife and children is only condoned (if it is) because he actually carried out his purpose of painting beautifully in Tahiti. Still, surely Kant is right that the careless driver, and Gauguin, count as behaving badly whatever the outcome.

9) Tendentiousness

Schopenhauer says that Kant purports to avoid preconceptions about 'the good' or goodness, and would like to convey that he is enjoining us to make our own laws out of reason. But he is guilty of 'self-mystification' about his motives and aims, and Christian values are smuggled in. He is like a man at a ball who spends the whole evening flirting with a masked beauty 'in the vain hope of making a conquest', until finally she throws off her mask and reveals herself as his wife.

Key points

- Kant caters for the double-sided, paradoxical nature of morality, its hyper-objectivity and hyper-subjectivity. It relies on freedom and yet is about laws. It asserts, and depends upon, objectivity and universality, and yet the individual's conscience (subjective and personal) is the final arbiter.

- He wants to find a law of morality that applies universally and necessarily to all beings that have reason.

- Reason cannot be designed by nature to achieve happiness, since instinct would be better at doing so. Its function must be to produce a good will, which is the only unqualifiedly good thing in, or even out of, the world.

- A good will is one that acts out of duty, and not from any other motive.

- To act out of duty is to act out of reverence for the moral law.

- The way to test whether I am acting out of reverence for the moral law is to look at the maxim (principle) under which I am acting.

- The principle under which I act must be one that can apply to everyone, not just to me.

- Hypothetical imperatives order you to do something only if you want something else.

- Categorical imperatives order you to do something because it is objectively necessary in itself, quite apart from its relation to a further end. They are concerned not with the action itself and its presumed results, but with its form and with the principle from which it follows.

- A will's goodness is in no way affected by whether the action that it wills has good or bad consequences.

- Kant says that everyone uses the categorical moral imperative in any case, but that having a philosophical formulation of it will help to avoid self-deception.

Glossary

Abstract idea
(According to Locke) the generalised concept that we extrapolate from our observation of regularly co-occurring clusters of qualities, and on the basis of which we classify them into things and species. (See Essence, real and nominal) Pooh-poohed by Berkeley.

Apperception
Leibniz's term for knowledge of our own mental states, the perception of perceiving. Kant postulates a transcendental unity of apperception – the oneness of consciousness that synthesises perceptions into experience had by me, but is not a knowable self.

A priori and a posteriori
A priori knowledge is knowledge that is independent of, not gained through, experience, and is 'necessary': no experience can disprove it. Rationalists claim that we are born with a priori knowledge of maths and moral values, for instance, though admittedly experience and teaching are required to activate it.

A posteriori knowledge is knowledge that is gained through experience, and is dependent on the variable way things have been, are, or will be; not necessarily, but contingently, true.

Archetype and ectype
An archetype is an original model or pattern. Each of Plato's Forms (Ideas) is an archetype that imparts to the particular things that imitate it their defining nature and identity (a bed is a bed, for instance, because it (partly) resembles the perfect Form of Bed). Berkeley's archetypes are ideas in the mind of God, of which human minds have copies (ectypes).

Atomism or corpuscular theory
Democritus in the 5th century BCE proposed that reality must ultimately be composed of indivisible particles, which constantly combine, disintegrate, and differently recombine. This theory of atomism solved the problem of the constancy of matter. Robert Boyle and other 17th century scientists called their very similar theory 'corpuscularianism' or 'the corpuscular theory' so as to distance it from what was regarded as pagan materialism.

Beg the question
To assume at the outset of argument precisely what you need to prove in, and through, arguing.

Cartesian dualism
The claim (explicitly made by Descartes, but much older) that reality, and everything in it, consists of two types of stuff – mental and physical.

Categorical moral imperative
In Kant's moral philosophy, the moral law that you freely impose upon yourself. Unlike a hypothetical (if-based) imperative (which depends on the action's aim and the agent's desires), a categorical imperative is unconditionally binding. The test for what it is permissible to do (in a particular case) is to ask yourself whether you would be willing for everyone else to be obliged to do it.

Clear and distinct idea
Descartes' frustratingly unclear and indistinct concept of an idea or intuition which, because informed by the natural light of reason, is too immediate, lucid and salient to be doubted, so can be taken as a touchstone for truth.

Compatibilism (See Determinism)
A range of views that see determinism and free will as reconcilable, holding that we count as being free as long as (or whenever) we can do what we want; while admitting that we only want what we want as the result of genes, conditioning and chance. It is just determinism rebranded, like calling a 'terrorist' a 'freedom fighter'.

Conatus
For Spinoza, the drive that each finite mode (entity) has to preserve itself in its own being – a drive that is its essence, and that can be seen alternately as the decision, or as the physical cause, that determines its activity.

Determinism (and free will)
Morality and social customs presuppose that we deliberately choose our actions, out of our own free will, and are therefore responsible for them. Science would suggest, and determinism claims,

that free will is an illusion since humans cannot be exempt from the causal laws that determine everything else in the universe.

Emotivism

The range of views (in moral philosophy) which hold that, because there are no moral facts or moral knowledge, and a moral judgment cannot therefore be true or false, it is really a disguised expression of approval or disapproval that is designed to influence and persuade. ('Stealing is wrong' in fact means 'Stealing: ugh!')

Empiricism

A way of philosophising which starts from the assumption that all knowledge is based on, and derived from, sensory experience. Empiricists claim we don't have innate ideas, though some treat maths and definitions as *a priori*.

Epistemology

The branch of philosophy that examines the nature and scope of what we can know, how we acquire knowledge, and whether knowledge is even possible in the first place.

Essence

The key and definitive attribute of a substance which makes that substance the sort of substance it is. Spinoza (on a subjectivist interpretation) says that substance *seems to have* more than one attribute which constitutes its essence, or (on an objectivist interpretation) that substance *actually does have* more than one essential attribute (either view being puzzling because of the uniqueness implied by 'essence').

Locke distinguishes between the nominal essence of a substance (the man-made classification, based on observed regularities, by which things are sorted into species) and its real essence (its true internal constitution, which the classification is supposedly based on, but which remains unknown).

Form

1) Translation mostly used for Plato's 'Idea' – the archetype that informs each member of a class of things.
2) The structure of a thing that makes it what it is.

Idealism

Should be 'idea-ism', as it concerns ideas, not ideals. A range of views which hold that reality consists of, or is constructed by, minds and/or mental representations. Subjective idealism (a view ascribed to Berkeley) starts with individual human consciousness. From the representationlist premise that all we directly perceive are our ideas, it argues to the conclusion that only what perceives, or is perceived, exists; there being no independently existing 'external world'. Transcendental idealism is Kant's theory that reality is only knowable as structured by our minds; things-in-themselves being forever ineluctably beyond our knowledge.

Immaterialism

A term (coined by Berkeley) that focuses on the negative aspect of idealism – its denial of material things – but is often used synonymously with it.

Impressions

Hume, considering 'ideas' too capacious a term, used 'impressions' for our immediate sensory perceptions, in contradistinction to the less vivid but more lasting 'ideas' (concepts) that are 'copied' from them. He doesn't commit himself as to whether our impressions are caused by qualities or things in the external world, and his position may amount to phenomenalism or idealism

Indirect Realism

The view that, although there is a real, independently-existing world, we can only perceive it indirectly, via our 'ideas' (sense data).

Induction

The method of reasoning that moves from repeated observations of the same type of thing or event to conclude a general law or principle about that type, and therefore a habitual present tense about its functioning or nature (for instance, water has always boiled at 100 degrees, therefore water boils at 100 degrees; all observed swans have been white, therefore all swans are white). Induction is liable to disproof, as in the latter case, and Hume famously questioned its rationality.

Intuition

1) The sense we use as a tuning-fork when philosophising to sound out what seems true or false or is disconsonant with our ingrained views. There is disagreement over how far we should rely on our intuitions, or override them (for instance, the intuition that it is wrong to kill someone for the sake of saving five others).
2) For Descartes, the same as a 'clear and distinct idea'.
3) For Kant, an element of raw sense perception as it would be if it were not already structured by the categories and the understanding. 'Pure intuitions' are those of space and time.

Mind body problem

The problem of how mental states are to be accommodated in a scientific account of the world. There have been constant claims that they are really nothing but brain states, or that mental terms are 'really' descriptions of behaviour, or even that the very category 'mental' is atavistic and superfluous. So far all such claims seem unworkable, and cannot convincingly account for subjectivity, that our experiences feel like something to us, and that our thinking is directed to things outside our firing neurons.

Mode
The modification that a substance goes through – being green in spring and gold in autumn, for instance. Spinoza's use of 'mode' covers not merely entities (within the unified substance that reality is) but also facts, events and relations.

Monism
Range of views which claim that reality, and everything in it, consists of only one type of stuff, whether this be mental (idealism) or physical (physicalism); or view (Spinoza) that reality only comprises one substance.

Moral luck
View that we do not (and for psychological and legal reasons, virtually cannot) assess an action purely in the light of the agent's intentions, but inevitably tend to take its consequences into account. Gauguin's selfishness in deserting his family seems less bad than it might have done had his paintings in Tahiti not been so good.

Moral rationalism
Views that morality originated in, and operates by means of, reason. Moral principles, moral facts or moral values (whichever features in the particular theory) are usually considered to be objective, absolute and knowable *a priori*, possibly installed in innate ideas, and are to be discerned and formulated through reasoning.

Naturalism
The view that everything is in principle explicable through scientific methods, and that our (natural) tendency to see humans as somehow other than, even above, nature is to be resisted.

Necessary connection
That a cause *has to* be followed by its effect – an assumed fact which (as Hume pointed out) we never have experience of, and which therefore, according to empiricism, *isn't* a fact. Hume sought to discredit, yet psychologically account for, our belief in 'necessary connection', thereby inspiring Kant's metaphysics.

Noumena (and phenomena)
Kant's term for the things-in-themselves, which – unmediated by our intuitions of space and time, and by the categories – we can never know. 'Phenomena' are things as we necessarily perceive them, that is, the noumena as structured by time, space and the categories.

Ontology
A field of metaphysics that is less concerned with the nature of reality as a whole, more with the specific entities that comprise it (although of course what these count as being will itself depend on what reality's overall nature is said to be).

Phenomenalism
Radical form of empiricism which holds that all we can know is our sense experience – what 17th and 18th century philosophers would call 'ideas' (or 'impressions'), and current philosophers would call 'sense data'. Phenomenalism is epistemological where idealism is metaphysical – and in some versions leaves it an open question as to whether there is an independently existing external world (beyond our knowledge).

Prescriptivism
A meta-ethical theory (originated by R.M. Hare) which, like emotivism, holds that a moral statement cannot be a factual statement, but claims instead that it is essentially both a commendation (or condemnation) and a special sort of command which entails that whoever issues it has to apply it to themselves as well as to everyone else.

Primary and secondary qualities
Primary qualities are qualities that an object is said to have quite independently of whether or not it is perceived – its shape, size, weight, movement or stillness, and number. They can be mathematically measured, and are accessible to two senses – sight and touch.

Secondary qualities are qualities (in objects) that, by interacting with our senses, systematically cause us to have ideas that do not actually resemble them – for instance, light-waves, which, interacting with our rods, cones and retinas, cause us to see colour.

(These terms were formulated by Locke, but Descartes had already expressed the concepts underlying them.)

Rationalism
A way of philosophising that, to varying degrees, privileges reason over sensory experience as the foundation and adjudicator of what is to count as knowledge.

Reflection

For Locke, sensation and reflection are the materials which, in tandem, 'furnish' us with knowledge. Reflection (rather like apperception) is the inner awareness of our mental operations. The term also seems to refer to the mental operations themselves, which, having stored in memory our passively produced ideas of sensation, then compare, combine and generalize these ideas.

Reification

'Res' is 'thing' in Latin. To reify is to treat some quality or concept that is (or may) *not be a thing* as if it definitely *is a thing* (for instance, self, a sense-datum, Nobody).

Representative theory of perception

The view that all we directly perceive are our own 'ideas' (sense-data), which are caused by the qualities of things outside the mind. For Locke, ideas are the exact copies of primary qualities, and are altered in systematic ways by the secondary qualities. It is unclear, though, how we can know whether our ideas resemble the qualities that cause them if these qualities, being themselves imperceptible, can never be compared with our ideas.

Scholasticism

The sort of philosophy practised in European universities, and by some Arabic and Jewish scholars, between the 10th and 17th centuries, which focussed on theology, language, logic, the problem of universals, interpretations of often badly-translated Aristotelean texts, and on squaring biblical with Ancient Greek authorities. 'Scholastic' came to epitomise dogmatism, obscurantism and logic-chopping.

Sense-data

The fragments of sensory experience – colour, sound, taste, texture, smell – which are conceived of (in the representative theory of perception) as forming a sort of mosaic that mentally represents the external world. We can also have hallucinatory sense data.

Sentimentalism

A view that arose at the beginning of the 18th century in reaction to moral rationalism. Sentimentalists such as Francis Hutcheson held that the practice of morality originated in, and continues to be motivated by, sentiment (particularly sympathy) rather than reason. For Hume, 'sympathy' is indeed the basis of morality, but he uses the term not for sympathy itself but for what he regards as facilitating it – the mental mechanism by which we automatically register and replicate the feelings of other people.

Simple and complex ideas

Simple ideas in the mind are, analogously to atoms in matter, the ultimate and basic units out of which knowledge is built (according to Locke). From simple ideas, each of which is caused by a primary or a secondary quality, the mind constructs complex ideas. Locke said that constantly co-occurring idea clusters are 'considered as united in one thing', which leaves open how optional or accurate such considering is.

Social contract theory

Range of views about the literal, or perhaps metaphorical, prerequisite for civil society – that humans first lived in a wild lawless condition but later made an agreement to sacrifice individual freedom in return for the peace, law and stability of being governed. For Locke (and for Rousseau in some moods), the 'state of nature' is relatively benign, but for Hobbes it is so terrifyingly predatory that virtually any regime is preferable.

Solipsism

The belief that only I and my experiences certainly exist – a belief that arises from taking immediate personal experience as the necessary foundation of knowledge: what could guarantee that there is anything outside my experience?

Substance

A concept originated by Aristotle for something that exists independently and persists through time while its properties and modes change. Spinoza declared that the only candidate for being a substance is God. Descartes said the same, but added that there also 'created substances' of two sorts – mental and physical. Locke's representative theory of perception forced him to prevaricate about what, if at all, substance could be. For Berkeley, there are only mental substances; for Hume, none at all. Kant said that, due to the way our minds structure experience, we have to discern substances in the world, whether or not there really are any.

Enlightenment Figures

Francis Bacon (c.1561–1626) Empiricist, scientist, statesman, essayist

Galileo Galilei (c.1564–1642) Scientist, heliocentrist

Thomas Hobbes (c.1588–1679) Political philosopher

Robert Filmer (c.1588–1653) Supporter of Divine Right of Kings

Marin Mersenne (c.1588–1648) Mathematician, polymath, friend of Descartes

Pierre Gassendi (c.1592–1655) Mathematician, astronomer, correspondent with Descartes

René Descartes (c.1596–1650) Dualist, rationalist, physicist, geometrician, mathematician

Pierre de Fermat (c.1601–1665) Probability theorist

Antoine Arnauld (c.1612–1694) Theologian, mathematician, friend of Descartes

Ralph Cudworth (c.1617–1688) Moral rationalist

Elisabeth of Bohemia (c.1618–1680) Descartes' philosophical correspondent

Anthony Ashley Cooper, 1st Earl of Shaftesbury (1621–1683) politician, Locke's patron

Blaise Pascal (c.1623–1662) Mathematician, scientist, essayist, famous for Pascal's Wager

Margaret Cavendish (c.1623–1673) Philosopher, poet

Arnold Geulincx (c.1624–1669) Flemish philosopher, follower of Descartes

Queen Christina (c.1626–1689) Descartes' philosophical pupil

Robert Boyle (c.1627–1691) Scientist, friend of Locke

Anne Conway, Viscountess Conway (c.1631–1679) Rationalist philosopher

Baruch Spinoza (c.1632–1677) Major rationalist philosopher

John Locke (c.1632–1704) Major empiricist, Political philosopher

Samuel von Pufendorf (c.1632–1694) Social contract theorist

Nicolas Malebranche (c.1638–1715) Occasionalist philosopher

Isaac Newton (c.1643–1727) Scientist, co-inventor of calculus

Gottfried Leibniz (c.1646–1716) Major rationalist, famous for windowless monads; co-inventor of calculus

Pierre Bayle (c.1647–1706) sceptic, author of the influential *Historical and Critical Dictionary*

John Toland (c.1670–1722) Irish political philosopher, controversial philosopher of religion

Giambattista Vico (c.1668–1744) Italian political philosopher, philosopher of history, proto-social scientist

Bernard Mandeville (c.1670–1733) political philosopher and economist, satirist

Christian Wolff (c.1679–1754) Rationalist philosopher, follower of Leibniz, influence on Kant

George Berkeley (c.1685–1753) Empiricist philosopher, immaterialist

Alexander Pope (c.1688–1744) Poet, satirist, friend of Berkeley

Charles de Secondat, Baron de Montesquieu (c.1689–1755) Political philosopher, famous for *The Spirit of the Laws* and *Persian Letters*

Joseph Butler (c.1692–1752) Philosopher, theologian, bishop

Voltaire (François-Marie Arouet) (c.1694–1778) Figure of the French Enlightenment, writer, philosopher, satirist

Francis Hutcheson (c.1694–1746) Sentimentalist moral philosopher, proto-utilitarian

John Wesley (c.1703–1791) Theologian and priest who co-founded Methodism

David Hartley (c.1705–1757) Philosopher of psychology and physiology

Emilie du Chatelet (c.1706–1749) Mathematician, physicist, translator of Newton

Julien de la Mettrie (c.1709–1751) Materialist philosopher, famous for *Man, the Machine*

Samuel (Dr) Johnson (c.1709–1784) Essayist, lexicographer, moralist, wit

Thomas Reid (c.1710–1796) Member of Scottish Enlightenment, founder of Scottish Common Sense philosophy

David Hume (c.1711–1776) Empirical philosopher, moral philosopher, essayist, historian

Jean-Jacques Rousseau (c.1712–1778) Political philosopher, influenced the cult of primitivism, educationalist, composer, economist

Denis Diderot (c.1713–1784) Figure of the French Enlightenment, philosopher, editor of the *Encyclopedia*, one-time friend of Rousseau

Etienne de Condillac (c.1714–1780) Epistemologist and philosopher of mind

Claude Adrien Helvétius (c.1715–1771) Philosopher of psychology and education, determinist, Encyclopedist

Jean d'Alembert (c.1717–1783) Mathematician, philosopher, scientist, co-editor with Diderot of the *Encyclopedia*

Baron d'Holbach (c.1723–1789) Philosopher, determinist, Encyclopedist, *salonniere*

Adam Smith (c.1723–1790) Economic theorist, member of Scottish Enlightenment

Immanuel Kant (c.1724–1804) Metaphysician, moral philosopher, philosopher of aesthetics

Moses Mendelssohn (c.1729–1786) Member of the Jewish Enlightenment, Kant's fellow-essayist

Gotthold Lessing (c.1729–1781) German philosopher, playwright and art critic

Edmund Burke (c.1729–1797) Political philosopher claimed by the Conservatives

Thomas Paine (c.1737 – 1809) Revolutionary political philosopher and activist, author of *Rights of Man*, influence on American Revolution

James Boswell (c.1740–1795) Scottish biographer, most famous for his biography of Samuel Johnson

Thomas Jefferson (c.1743–1826) Political philosopher claimed by the Liberals

William Paley (c.1743–1805) Philosopher, Christian apologist, clergyman

Nicolas de Caritat, Marquis de Condorcet (c.1743–1794) Political philosopher and mathematician

Jeremy Bentham (c.1748–1832) Moral philosopher, founder of Utilitarianism

Johann Goethe (c.1749–1832) Novelist, playwright, poet

Dugald Stewart (c.1753–1828) Scottish moral philosopher

William Godwin (c.1756–1836) Political philosopher, novelist, anarchist, Wollstonecraft's husband

Maximilien Robespierre (c.1758–1794) Lawyer and politician, key figure in the French Revolution and the Reign of Terror

Mary Wollstonecraft (c.1759–1797) Philosopher, feminist, author of *A Vindication of the Rights of Woman*, mother of Mary Shelley

Friedrich Schiller (c.1759–1805) Romantic philosopher and playwright

Johann Gottlieb Fichte (c.1762–1814) Philosopher, founder of German Idealism

(Madame) Germaine de Stael (c.1766–1817) Woman of letters, *salonniere*

Index

Picture Credits

Alamy: *61 (René Magritte ©ADAGP, Paris and DACS, London 2018)*
British Museum: *128*
Getty Images: *143 (Archive Photos/Stringer)*
Metropolitan Museum of Art: *8 (The Elisha Whittelsey Collection, The Elisha Whittelsey Fund, 1962), 9 (Harris Brisbane Dick Fund, 1917)*
Shutterstock: *34, 35, 36, 48, 91, 93, 115, 117, 121, 125, 131, 136, 138, 145, 152, 154, 155, 173, 185, 211, 225*
Wellcome Collection: *11, 14, 17, 27, 38, 40, 46, 49, 53, 55, 64, 77, 80, 94, 97, 98, 102, 111, 118, 126, 150, 151, 160, 191, 195, 215, 221*